Advance Praise for *Moving the Mountain*

"Imam Feisal . . . is an inspirational and erudite exponent for the Muslim world. This tale of his journey is a clarion call for a progressive and pluralistic Islam as a bedrock of tolerance and understanding. Believers and adherents of all faiths must stand in solidarity with this global spiritual leader whose cry for religious freedom and human dignity must be heard."

—Rabbi Marc Schneier (president) and Russell Simmons (chairman),
The Foundation for Ethnic Understanding

"Inspiring, honest, and insightful, *Moving the Mountain* crosses the bridge from East to West and demonstrates the vital role that American Muslims can play in strengthening the voice of religious moderation across the world. Imam Feisal eloquently reminds us that women's rights, religious harmony, and equality for all are core values embedded in Islam, and he challenges us to confidently embrace that mandate today."

—Her Majesty Queen Noor Al Hussein of Jordan

"In this thoughtful book, Imam Feisal explores the need to create an American Muslim community that fits in with the nation's traditions of pluralism and tolerance . . . an important contribution to understanding Islam and the struggle against extremism."

—Walter Isaacson, bestselling author of *Steve Jobs*
and president of the Aspen Institute

"Feisal Abdul Rauf is a name that one day should come as easily to the lips as do the names of Martin Luther King Jr. and Gandhi. It is my hope that when my fellow Americans read this incredibly moving and enlightening book they will feel the scales of ignorance and fear falling off their eyes. With gentleness and love, [Imam Feisal] seeks to bring us all together in post-9/11 America."

—Michael Moore

"In our post-9/11 world, where a gulf of fear and suspicion too often separates American Muslims from other Americans, Imam Feisal Abdul Rauf is an ideal ambassador: an immigrant to America, a defender of its principles, and a believer that people of diverse backgrounds and faiths can thrive within its borders. With *Moving the Mountain,* Rauf has put his gift of storytelling in service of the empathy that all of us—Muslims and non-Muslims alike—so desperately need."

—Arianna Huffington

"Everybody should read this book. It shows us the dangers of our past course and where we should be aiming."

—Karen Armstrong, bestselling author of *Islam: A Short History* and *Muhammad, A Prophet for Our Time*

"An authentic voice, an essential vision, a heartfelt story. *Moving the Mountain* can—and should—move America."

—James Carroll, bestselling author of *Constantine's Sword* and *Jerusalem, Jerusalem.*

"An erudite and insightful look into the future of Islam and America, identifying those values that could bridge differences between Muslims, Christians, and Jews. A book about how religion can bring people together, heal wounds, and show a future of hope and coexistence."

—Vali Nasr, bestselling author of *The Shia Revival* and *The Rise of Islamic Capitalism*

"Imam Feisal is arguably the most influential Muslim leader in America. His bold vision of a moderate, pluralistic, and distinctly American Islam is something that all Americans should champion."

—Reza Aslan, bestselling author of *No god but God* and *Beyond Fundamentalism*

"Imam Feisal's voice is one that Americans and Muslim's world-wide need to hear. . . . He teaches an authentic and beautiful Islam, and demonstrates just how compatible his religion is with core American values."

—James Zogby, president of the Arab American Institute and author of *Arab Voices: What They Are Saying to Us and Why It Matters*

"Imam Feisal personifies the most noble and sublime teachings of Islam that seek to advance the well-being, happiness, and flourishing of all people. At a time when religion is tragically and violently hijacked by those who desecrate its name, the need to hearken to his articulate voice is greater than ever."

—Rabbi David Rosen, Interfaith Advisor to the Chief Rabbinate of Israel

"Imam Feisal has one of the most reasoned, elegant voices in Islam today. It's very urgent for Americans to read what this thoughtful, careful man really has to tell us."

—Rev. Dr. Joan Brown Campbell, Director of Religion
at the Chautauqua Institution

"*Moving the Mountain* is wise, authentic, and courageous. Every American needs to read this transforming and spiritually insightful book about the profound hope American Islam offers the world."

—Rabbi Irwin Kula, President of The National Jewish Center
for Learning and Leadership

ALSO BY IMAM FEISAL ABDUL RAUF

What's Right with Islam: A New Vision for Muslims and the West

Islam—A Sacred Law: What Every Muslim Should Know About the Shariah

Islam: A Search for Meaning

MOVING THE MOUNTAIN

Beyond Ground Zero to a New Vision of Islam in America

Imam Feisal Abdul Rauf

Free Press
New York London Toronto Sydney New Delhi

*f*P

Free Press
A Division of Simon & Schuster, Inc.
1230 Avenue of the Americas
New York, NY 10020

First Free Press hardcover edition May 2012

Designed by Carla Jayne Jones

Manufactured in the United States of America

1 3 5 7 9 10 8 6 4 2

Library of Congress Cataloging-in-Publication Data

Abdul Rauf, Feisal
Moving the mountain : beyond ground zero to a new vision of Islam in America / Feisal Abdul Rauf.
p. cm.
Includes bibliographical references.
1. Islam—United States. 2. Muslims—United States. I. Title.
BP67.U6A238 2012
297.0973—dc23 2011050797

ISBN 978-1-4516-5600-8
ISBN 978-1-4516-5602-2 (ebook)

To people of all beliefs struggling to reclaim moderate, nonviolent religion and politics from the grasp of extremism—and heal our broken world

Had Muhammad not gone to the mountain, the mountain would have come to Muhammad.

—Proverb

For truly I tell you, if you have faith the size of a mustard seed, you will say to this mountain, "Move from here to there," and it will move; and nothing will be impossible for you.

—Matthew 17:20

God is our refuge and strength, a very present help in trouble. Therefore we will not fear, though the earth should change, though the mountains shake in the heart of the sea; though its waters roar and foam, though the mountains tremble with its tumult.

—Psalm 46:1–3

CONTENTS

AUTHOR'S NOTE

In this book I quote frequently from the Quran, the holy scripture of Islam, the authoritative text of which is in Arabic. Whenever I quote the Quran directly, I identify the chapter (in Arabic, the *sura*) and, after a colon, the verse, as in Quran 2:146. There are literally dozens of English translations of the Quran. I have tried to cite those that are truest to the letter and spirit of the original Arabic. On occasion, however, when I am dissatisfied with the common translation, I have provided my own, as in my translation of the Muslim statement of faith, the *shahada,* on page 29. At the back of the book I have also provided a glossary of important Arabic terms used in the text.

Muslim belief, law, and practice are also based on the *Hadith,* the contemporary reports of the sayings and actions of the Prophet Muhammad. When I refer to an individual *hadith,* I do not capitalize the word; when I refer to more than one, I add an "s" to make the plural: *hadith*s. When I refer to the entire corpus of these reports, they are called, collectively, the *Hadith*. The *Hadith* consists of a variety of collections, which are normally identified by the last name of the compiler and a number given to each *hadith* in his compilation, as in Bukhari 2954, which refers to *hadith* number 2954 in the collection of Sahih al-Bukhari.

For quotations from the Hebrew Bible as well as the Gospels, I have generally used the New Revised Standard Version and have used the standard form of biblical citation: the name of the book, the number of the chapter, and, after the colon, the number of the verse, as in Deuteronomy 6:5–9.

Some key Muslim jurisprudential rulings or other sources are also identified in the text by their authors and books. These sources remain, for the most part, untranslated from classical Arabic. Knowing the author, book, and number will allow the reader to locate the rulings in these sources. Readers interested in the sources for other quotations or statistics or events will find them in endnotes keyed to the page in the text.

INTRODUCTION

In the past half-century an extremist version of Islam untrue to Muslim history and profoundly dangerous to Muslims and non-Muslims all over the world has tried to hijack the faith of 1.6 billion people, making it seem parochial, judgmental, narrow, self-righteous, and violent. By "extremist Islam" I mean a militant intolerance for differing points of view, which leads to denying others the right to their own opinions and potentially their freedom and humanity. Religious extremists insist that their interpretation of God, or God's will, is the only acceptable one, and that all who disagree are, in effect, heretics or unbelievers. Similarly, political extremism equates all dissent with disloyalty and treason. Regarding those who differ as infidels or traitors, extremists find it far easier to marginalize, abuse, jail, torture, or murder them.

Authentic Islam, in contrast, recognizes other religions' route to God; it is a religion of spirituality, compassion, and mercy rather than of judgment and punishment; its spirituality is elaborated in jurisprudential reasoning rather than emotional fanaticism; it prizes flexibility and adaptability to different cultures rather than rigid adherence to medieval mores.

By reclaiming Islam as a modern, moderate, compassionate, just, open, tolerant, and nonviolent religion, protective both of individual freedoms and collective human rights, this book seeks to move a mountain of suspicion, myth, fear, and hatred—and provide a new vision for Islam in America and the world. In articulating this understanding of Islam above all as a moderate, nonviolent religion, *Moving the Mountain* shows how Islam in America—and in particular *the emergence of an American Islam*—can and will play a vital role in waging the battle against religious and political extremism, the chief threat to American security and world peace today.

This book will show why it is so important to reclaim religious and political discourse from the extremists of all faiths who dominate so many of the headlines. As citizens of the most powerful country on earth, we Americans have immense influence; it is critical that we provide moderate global leadership in these dangerous times.

In these pages, non-Muslims will discover an Islam they hoped existed but feared did not. After all, the Islam as presented all over the Internet appears extreme, judgmental, rigid, and foreign to most American eyes, and television images of Iranian crowds chanting, "God is Great. Death to America," do not inspire tolerance or trust. The Islam that I practice is the faith the great majority of Muslims practice; it is very different from the extremist religion of current headlines. Hewing to fundamental principles of Islam reaching back fourteen centuries, to the time of the Prophet Muhammad, to his teachings, to the precedents of his companions, and to what centuries of scholars have taught, it offers moderation in theology, in jurisprudence, in governance, and in politics, as well as in matters of culture, gender relations, and worship.

In these pages Muslims will find help reclaiming the authentic teachings of their faith from those who have misunderstood, distorted, and manipulated it and made Islam appear violent and archaic. They will take pleasure, I believe, in learning more about the compassionate wisdom of the Prophet, who explicitly warned his followers against the dangers of excessive religiosity (Nasa'i 3006). They will be surprised, if not shocked, to discover how much of what they believe to be Islamic is part of a continuum with our predecessor faiths, and they will receive concrete help in adapting their religion to an American context.

Islam is already part of this country; it is no longer just a foreign import. A vibrant, assertive, unapologetic, nonviolent, moderate, thoroughly American Islam will both further enrich our culture and society and play a critical role worldwide in the battle against religious and political extremism proclaimed in the name of Islam.

We live in troubled times. Wars rage, the Earth warms, and mountains tremble; waters of all kinds "roar and foam." There is surely a good bit of heavy lifting ahead of us, and yet, according to the proverb and Jesus in the epigraphs that open this book, there is no mountain that faith cannot move. I cannot claim, as Martin Luther King Jr. did the night before he was killed, to have gone "up to the mountain" and to have "seen the Promised Land." I have caught glimpses of it, however: in the sight of the Statue of Liberty when I was a seventeen-year-old coming to this country, in interfaith worship in Tahrir Square in Cairo in the middle of a revolution, in the speeches of American leaders affirming Muslims' rights as Americans, in the pained wisdom of 9/11 families, in the embraces of rabbis and ministers, and in the American Muslim wedding of a young Bosnian woman and a young Senegalese man. Like King, I believe that "we, as a people, will get to the Promised Land." I hope this book will help us get there.

My Tradition

Like the great majority of the world's Muslims, I am an orthodox Muslim, neither an "Islamist" nor a "radical jihadist." By "orthodox" I mean the authentic mainstream, moderate, nonviolent religion practiced by the vast preponderance of Muslims since the days of the Prophet. Orthodox Islam is a powerful, deep, beautiful, ancient and modern, wisdom-based, justice-seeking religion. Adhering to core principles of faith, practice, and ethics, Muslim scholars, thinkers, and jurists led the way from the earliest times in creatively expressing their faith in the vernacular of the cultures in which they found themselves: the countries surrounding the Arabian peninsula where Islam was born, known as the "cradle of civilization," including the ancient and highly developed nations of Egypt, Babylon and Mesopotamia (modern Iraq), Byzantium (modern Turkey), Persia (modern Iran), Abyssinia (modern Ethiopia), and India.

Muslims routinely incorporated pre-Islamic institutions, laws, and customs into their practice when these did not go against the teachings of our scripture, the Quran, or the Prophet's directives. Nor over the centuries did Muslim thinkers simply and blindly seek to re-create seventh-century Arabia, when the Prophet Muhammad walked the earth. Instead they avidly responded to the Prophet's urging them to "seek knowledge, even as far as China."

Within two centuries after the Prophet's death, by the mid-ninth century, Muslims had translated every book they could get their hands on from throughout the known world, from Greece in the West to China in the East. These were all housed in the Baghdad library known as the House of Wisdom. Following the Prophet's dictum that knowledge is our inheritance wherever we find it, Muslims embraced the religious, spiritual, legal, scientific, technological, and architectural achievements of all the peoples they came across, incorporated this knowledge into the Islamic heritage, and between the eighth and eleventh centuries, with their own creative and inventive contributions, built the greatest civilization then in the world—what has become known as the Islamic civilization.

Drawing on the Quran and the *Hadith,* Muslim theologians and jurists developed an Islamic theology and jurisprudence incorporating wisdom from the predecessor religions of Judaism and Christianity and their texts, commentaries, spiritual practices, theology, and jurisprudence. The cross-fertilization of Greek philosophy with Roman and Mesopotamian jurisprudence helped shape Islamic jurisprudence and law. The Roman *prudent,* who would issue a legal opinion to educate his townsfolk on an issue of law, became in the Islamic context the mufti, who would issue fatwas (legal opinions consistent with Islamic law) to help his constituency understand Islamic legal determinations of right and wrong.

The spires of Christian churches calling the pious with ringing bells metamorphosed into tall minarets from which the muezzin would call the faithful to prayer. And the distinctive dome of the Byzantine Orthodox cathedral Hagia Sophia, built between 532 and 537 (more than thirty years before the birth of the Prophet), was adopted by Muslims, first as the Dome of the Rock and later by the Ottoman architect Sinan, so much so that the dome became a ubiquitous feature of most later mosques. Too many of today's Muslims subscribe to the notion that Islamic civilization came into being entirely sui generis, as though Muslims had no intellectual or spiritual forebears. The truth is that in every field of knowledge and culture, Muslims translated, absorbed, integrated, and built upon the achievements and knowledge of their predecessors.

The past half-century has fostered the myth among Muslims that all knowledge other than that contained in the Quran and the sayings of the Prophet is "un-Islamic." But 1,400 years of Islamic history show us that the true Muslim reality is an enlightened tradition of seeking out, engaging, embracing, absorbing, and extending knowledge and wisdom in all fields of human endeavor from all over the world.

An American Journey

I am an American citizen born in Kuwait of Egyptian parents. I grew up in Great Britain, Malaysia, and Egypt and have lived in the United States since 1965, when I was seventeen. I attended Columbia University in New York and graduate school at the Stevens Institute of Technology in New Jersey, and I became a naturalized American citizen in 1979. I am an imam, which means literally "the person who leads the prayer," and the son of an eminent Egyptian imam and scholar who was sent by al-Azhar University in Cairo, the preeminent Islamic seminary in the Muslim world, to be the imam and director of the Islamic Center in New York, and then of the Islamic Center in Washington, D.C. Since 1983 I have served at the al-Farah Mosque in Tribeca, about a dozen blocks from the former World Trade Center. Like my father, I have been deeply involved in multifaith work; I have worked for well over a quarter-century with all faith communities, but mainly with Jews, Christians, and Buddhists.

This enlightened tradition is also America's tradition, the America symbolized by the Statue of Liberty that has been welcoming, incorporating, and integrating people of different cultures (not without difficulties and conflict, I know) for centuries. I have lived this experience myself, here in New York City.

But until I understood and assimilated all this, I experienced serious culture shock after I arrived in America. For someone with a religious upbringing, the 1960s were an extremely difficult time. Even though religion was a big part of the civil rights and peace movements, in my college religion was treated as irrelevant, hopelessly stodgy, and behind the times. This was the heyday of the "God is dead" movement. Islam was almost always portrayed negatively in the media and larger culture. Most American Muslims were Black Muslims, members of the separatist Nation of Islam headed by Elijah Muhammad, of which most whites were terrified. Arabs were then considered uncouth, dirty, and uncivilized.

In Malaysia, where Western culture was extremely influential, I'd grown up listening to Elvis and the Beatles and watching American movies. People wanted to be like Americans. In contrast, when I got here, I saw prosperous middle-class American college students wanting to somehow join the Third World. I understood their anger about the military draft and the Vietnam War, but their talking and singing about revolution and idolizing Che Guevara and Fidel Castro made no sense to me at all.

Add my own search for identity to this mix, and the freedom that was everywhere—in the form of drugs, sex, and alcohol—was unnerving, to say the least. Staying chaste until marriage, a commandment of my faith, was one of the most difficult challenges of my young life. I had a powerful sense that if I did not get a grip on my identity, my ethics, and my religion, I would go off the rails. I was confronting the very meaning of my life.

For the first time in my life I had to *decide* whether, and to what extent, to be a Muslim. In a Muslim society like Egypt or Malaysia, practicing your faith is like observing Christmas for many in America: you do it almost without thinking, because it is part of the environment. But in the morally free maelstrom of the 1960s, trying to be religious by choice required enormous effort. America made it possible for me to feel the misery of being someone without an identity. But finally, using that very individual freedom for which American culture is so rightly celebrated, I was able to consciously and deliberately choose the religion I had grown up with.

For the next several years Islam helped structure my life—which was badly in need of some structure—as well as my personal relationship with God. I was the kind of person who needed coherent rational understanding of what I was experiencing. As a physics major, I needed to put everything together into an integrated whole, a kind of Grand Unified Theory of my life, so I began to read books on religion, philosophy, and theology.

As the oldest son of an eminent scholar, I had also learned a great deal from my father. I had learned to type at age twelve (on a now long obsolete Royal mechanical typewriter), first typing my father's thesis, and then his lectures, radio talks, and sermons. Reading what I was typing, I would ask him pointed questions that expressed my doubts as much as my need to be convinced of the truth of my inherited faith. In reading the Quran, I saw how God criticized those who blindly followed the religion of their fathers (Quran 2:170). And since I prided myself on being a good thinker, I felt that if I practiced Islam just because it was my father's religion, I was opening myself to the same criticism. I therefore had to adopt Islam based on my own genuine conviction, and I needed to have something substantial to build on if I was to adopt it sincerely at all. Learning Islam intellectually was different from feeling or experiencing this religion as my own choice, but a no less important part of integrating the whole gestalt of being a Muslim.

I worked hard to put myself together in those years, to reconfigure myself in a way that was true to my own deepest principles. I had to confront and absorb the meaning of my religion, its spiritual core as well as its ethical imperatives. How was I to deal with the drugs and alcohol that surrounded me, the free and open sexuality seemingly celebrated everywhere? How was I to relate to other people, Muslims as well as non-Muslims, to Jews in the wake of the 1967 and 1973 wars between Israel and my home country of Egypt? What about the racism I saw everywhere, and experienced directly and frequently? What to make of friends who were very different, who engaged easily in premarital sex, who smoked marijuana, who were gay?

What helped me through this period was to reflect on the fact that throughout my life, I had changed rapidly and continually in just about every way: physically, emotionally, and intellectually. My body had changed every few years since my birth. Starting at the age of six, when every English boy's ambition was to be a train engineer, I found myself answering the question "What do you want to be when you grow up, Feisal?" differently every couple of years: a movie actor, then a director, then a musician, and then, at thirteen, a scientist. My emotional attachments followed a similar roller-coaster ride. At just seven years old I had such a crush on my teacher that I felt jilted when she married. Then every couple of years or so I would have a crush on another girl, without whom I felt I would not be able to live. It was painful to feel as though someone had invaded my heart and plucked out the love and passion I had felt just days earlier.

And yet, in spite of all these changes, in every measurable part of me I somehow knew I was the same person, the same Feisal—the same "I." This deep conviction, combined with my spiritual search for, journey to, and personal discovery of God, made me recognize that my soul—and its values and needs—was the truly permanent part of my being. The very changeability of everything else demonstrated to me the need to have something about my life that was indeed permanent, starting with my deepest values and ethics.

In time I came to understand the wisdom and rationale of my faith and developed answers to the most important of these questions, until at the age of twenty-five I felt I had done it: I had constructed an anchored spiritual, religious, and ethical worldview. I found my religion in America, freely and deliberately. It was my choice. I was deeply happy with it—as well as relieved that this internal struggle was over.

In the next ten years I held a job, focused on earning a living, married a beautiful American of Greek Irish Catholic background, and we had premature twin girls. Then my worldly life disintegrated. Six weeks after the twins were born, my wife and I both suffered serious illnesses that challenged our marriage. We were both twenty-nine years old. Despite strong efforts to keep the marriage intact, we separated three years later, and in another year my wife and I divorced. The heartbreak of a love lost, of a family broken, was a pain that was to live with me forever. But I had loved, and loved intensely. Even with the sense of a paradise lost, I could remember the heavenly feeling of being in love and therefore sought to love again.

I also learned that, in the hubris of my youth, what I thought I had accomplished spiritually was just one cycle of inner development. I had much more to learn, much further to grow in spiritual and human wisdom, for the process of inner development is never-ending. Most important, I had to learn to be humble in all aspects of life. The greatest spiritual and moral danger is that of the ego, which makes us believe we are more than we are. Control of the ego, the greatest source of evil in a human being, was my greatest challenge, and the greatest challenge that most people face. That is why I focused on my spiritual journey and discipline.

As part of the religious discipline I had undertaken, I took time off from my work in New Jersey and attended the noon Friday prayers at One Riverside Drive, at the Islamic Center of New York, where I had lived during my teenage years from 1965 to 1971. It was then the closest mosque to where I worked, just across the Hudson River, and I usually found free parking—no small consideration in New York City. But in the early 1980s my friend Muhtar Holland kept badgering me to attend another mosque, in downtown Manhattan; the spiritual leader there was an eminent Sufi from Istanbul named Sheikh Muzaffar Ozak, whose book *Guidance* my friend was translating into English. The mosque was then at 155 Mercer Street, just south of Houston Street, in the neighborhood New Yorkers know as SoHo.

The sheikh had a following here in the United States, and twice a year he would come from Turkey for six weeks at a time. So on Good Friday 1983—I had the day off since it was a holiday—and because parking was free on Good Friday, I took my daughters with me to the mosque downtown, Masjid al-Farah, or al-Farah Mosque. Sha'ban, the Turkish gentleman who volunteered as imam, invited me to give the call to prayer (known as the *adhan*). There were hardly a half-dozen people there. He loved my recitation of the *adhan*—whose magic is in that combination of chant, pronunciation, cadence, and spirituality that emerges from a feeling of surrender to God—which touched him so much that he pleaded with me, "You must come every week."

I did not want to. It was farther from my office; parking alone was absurdly expensive. And for what? To call the *adhan* for six people in a cavernous 4,000-square-foot room? But God has a way of intervening when it is His will. The following night I attended a monthly religious meeting at the Indonesian consulate. Since there were no Malay or Indonesian restaurants in the city at that time, I went mostly for the food, but also to keep up my Malay language skills (Malay and Indonesian are the same language) and to assuage a certain nostalgia for my boyhood. During the discussion that evening, a point of contention arose that required me to check my *Hadith* references. At home the next morning, as I opened my *Hadith* reference book, it fell open to the chapter "On the Excellence of Calling the Prayer." It was as though I felt a tap on my shoulder—and I recognized the sign: God wanted me to accept Sha'ban's plea that I be the muezzin at Masjid al-Farah.

And so I did. The very next week Sheikh Muzaffar himself arrived, and I went to the mosque with great anticipation. As I entered the second-floor room where he was seated in an armchair, speaking to a full house, our eyes locked and we shared a gaze of almost primordial recognition. As he was walking past me to leave later that evening, he stopped and put his hands in his pocket, fishing for something. I knew he was looking for something to give me, and we communicated without speaking, as a Sufi master I had met some years earlier instructed me to do. We smiled at each other, and I silently told him, "You really don't have to." With great kindness, he handed me a symbol of what we had already shared spiritually and of what he was bequeathing me: what Sufis call a "gift of transmission." It was not a spiritual amulet, or prayer beads, or his white cap (which he gave me six months later) or shawl. It was a roll of Tums—a sign perhaps to remain calm in the face of future challenges.

The following October, after returning from vacation, I had a phone message that Sheikh Muzaffar urgently wanted to meet with me. At our meeting he told me he wanted to appoint me imam of the mosque, responsible for leading the prayers and delivering the Friday sermons. I felt the rightness, even the spiritual imperative of the offer, and I accepted. (There are no ordained clergy in Islam.) I delivered my first sermon in Masjid al-Farah on the Friday of Thanksgiving 1983, and I still remember the unseasonably early snow that day as I drove to New York. In the Arab world, where water is so precious, rain is considered a blessing from God. I had a similar feeling about the snow. And parking turned out to be easy.

Two years later, in 1985, our congregation moved to its current location at 245 West Broadway in Tribeca, where we grew and grew, filling the ground floor of the building during Friday prayers. Two decades after our move, the congregation was using all the floors in the building and still we were bursting at the seams. By 2007 we were conducting three prayer services in succession on Fridays. We desperately needed a larger space.

My work as imam was spiritually and practically satisfying as well as challenging. It brought me great joy for many reasons. Most of all, it led me to Daisy Khan, whom I met, fell in love with, and married in 1996.

Over those decades I came to understand that what I had done for myself personally had become even more necessary in larger social and political terms. There were growing numbers of Muslims like me, seeking to reconcile their Muslim identities, and often their immigrant identities, with their lives and identities as Americans. They needed help understanding why and how America expressed many of the same values as the Quran, and why they had nothing to apologize for—to their families in Muslim-majority countries all over the world—in being Muslims who were authentically American.

In order to address these very issues on a much larger scale, in 1997 Daisy and I founded the American Society for Muslim Advancement (ASMA). We intended both to accelerate the process of shaping an American Islamic identity and to help anchor this identity in a spiritually authentic tradition and intellectually rigorous classical and orthodox understanding of Islam—something I felt was essential to our being well-rooted both in God and in our adopted country.

While we could see that an American Islamic identity was taking form naturally, as a matter of course and therefore haphazardly, we also thought that by being more deliberate—by being aware of how this happened in the context of other American immigrant faith communities, and in our own Islamic history—we could speed up the process. We could focus on being role models for future generations and help immigrant Muslims in America to become American *Muslims* (so that we are still seen by global Muslims as part of the global Muslim community, or *ummah*) and Muslim *Americans* (so that we are seen by our fellow Americans as loyal Americans true to what it means to be an American).

Equally important, we would build substantial bridges between Muslims and other religious believers. It was already becoming clear to me that the majority of Muslims were "culturally Muslim" but knew relatively little about their own faith: its history, its theology, its spirituality, and the vision these provided for understanding among different faiths. (In that sense they were no different from people of other faiths, most of whom know little about their religions either.)

I believed then, and continue to believe, like my father before me, that honest, candid dialogue among people of different faiths, leading to multifaith alliances acting together on issues of common concern and interest, is crucial to healing divisions in New York City and will help it shine as the model for a peaceful, tolerant, and increasingly globalized world. For as the most religiously diverse city in the world, New York City is a microcosm of the global village and demonstrates, day in and day out, how millions of people of different faiths and cultures may coexist peacefully. How we American Muslims integrate ourselves into the rich multifaith culture of New York City and the United States as a whole has consequences for Muslims throughout the world.

The Rise of Extremism at Home and Abroad

The 1980s and 1990s saw the rapid rise of religious fundamentalism and extremism across religious traditions that blended into new and existing religious nationalisms, the latter phenomenon starting with the birth of the Islamic Republic of Pakistan in 1947 and the Jewish State of Israel in 1948. While both states were markedly secular through the 1970s, religious fundamentalism and extremism took off in the 1980s.

One marker of this fundamentalism was the 1979 Iranian Revolution, which toppled the very secular, despotic shah and replaced his dictatorship with an Islamic republic whose first year was marked by holding Americans hostage in their own embassy for a year. The mujahedeen (precursors of the Taliban) in Afghanistan soon followed, supported by the CIA and the Pakistanis to combat the Soviet invasion of Afghanistan. The strategy of using religion for political gain worked. It worked for those who wanted power in Iran, and it worked for the U.S.-Saudi Arabia-Pakistan partnership in evicting the Soviets from Afghanistan and helping to implode the Soviet Union in 1989.

It also worked for Christian fundamentalists in the United States, who during the Reagan, Bush, and Clinton administrations were able to deploy religion and religious arguments to achieve their political agendas. Christian extremist acts in the United States—such as the murder of abortion providers—increased. Jewish extremism too grew into a powerful force in Israel: Israeli Prime Minister Yitzhak Rabin was murdered in 1995 by a Jewish extremist furious at Rabin's having signed the Oslo peace accords with the Palestinians. Politicians learned the power of radical religion, and fundamentalists and extremists basked in their newfound influence.

As if that were not enough, Samuel Huntington's notorious "clash of civilizations" idea in his seminal 1993 *Foreign Affairs* article and bestselling book three years later widely broadcast the idea that the Muslim world—the Islamic civilization that I found such a source of personal meaning and dignity—was the new enemy of the West! He influenced countless opinion leaders in universities, media outlets, and think tanks, and ratcheted up anti-Muslim feeling at all levels of the U.S. government and culture. Radical ideology—in this case an implicit declaration of war by America against the Muslim world—was heard loud and clear by Muslims. No doubt Osama bin Laden heard it, as did numerous intellectuals and Muslim world leaders. Radical ideology, especially when extremists act on that ideology, too often begets an oppositional force that is no less radical.

Terrorist attacks by extremist Muslims on the World Trade Center in 1993, the U.S. embassies in Kenya and Tanzania in 1998, and the USS *Cole* in 2000 bore witness to these growing, increasingly lethal tensions.

All of these developments came to a catastrophic head on September 11, 2001, as extremist Muslim fanatics planned and executed the largest terrorist attack in the history of the United States. Millions of Americans felt personally attacked by Islam itself and suspected all Muslims of being potential terrorists.

As Ground Zero smoldered in the days and weeks after 9/11, I was invited to speak to many organizations, religious as well as secular, about my faith. As the imam of a mosque just a dozen blocks from Ground Zero, I was in demand as a speaker on extremists and terrorists, on the relationship between the Muslim world and the West, helping non-Muslim Americans understand the nature of the divide.

Typically I would begin by describing the beliefs and worship of Muslims, and then open the floor to questions. These invariably fell into three categories: first was the "What is Islam?" class of questions, such as, What is the difference between Sunni, Shia, and Sufi? What is the role of women in Islam? Does Islam believe in separation of church and state? The second category was what I called "the 9/11 questions," such as, Why is Osama bin Laden popular among some in the Muslim world? Why are some Muslims so angry at America? Why do political liberation movements in the Muslim world use the language of Islam? Is suicide bombing allowed in Islam?

The third category contained just one question, and while I succeeded in answering the questions in the first two categories, my efforts to provide answers to the third left me deeply dissatisfied.

After 9/11: Healing the U.S.-Muslim Divide—Fighting Extremism Concretely

This third question first cropped up when my friend Rabbi David Rosen invited me to address the quarterly board of governors meeting of the American Jewish Committee on December 10, 2001—ninety days after 9/11. Members of the audience unanimously agreed with me that the status quo between Jews and Muslims was unacceptable. But they went further; they pushed me to state what we could do together to improve this relationship, and specifically what we could do to turn around U.S.-Muslim world relations.

I talked generally on mutually educating each other about our religions and cultures, which I knew was necessary. At the same time, I knew cultural and religious appreciation could not by itself transform a relationship that had gone very wrong. Necessary, yes. Sufficient? Not at all. A month later, at a lecture I gave at the Greenwich (Connecticut) Presbyterian Church, a kind lady stood up and asked me, "What can a good Christian woman like me do to help improve U.S.-Muslim relations?" Here again was the same question, this time posed by a devout Christian who wanted to put her efforts behind an initiative that would really turn around U.S.-Muslim relations—and I could not answer it! And if I could not, who could? This hugely important question stayed with me for months. I knew I had to do some serious studying and thinking.

In effect, 9/11 demanded that I recast what I had been doing first on a personal level, then in my mosque and at ASMA, to a national and international scale: try to defuse tensions and build connections between the global Muslim community and the American and Western multicultural, multifaith reality. I soon realized that to resolve the problems that people referred to as "Muslims versus the West" or "the U.S.-Muslim divide," we all needed something concrete that Christians and Jews, together with Muslims and other faith communities, could do together to help bridge the growing polarization between America and the Muslim world, and between Muslim Americans and their non-Muslim neighbors. This work needed to happen at the level of governments, religious institutions, academic institutions, think tanks, NGOs, businesses, media, and civil society. The scope of it was daunting.

I spent more than a year analyzing the problems and figuring out what it would take to bridge the so-called West-Muslim divide, what finite issues needed to be addressed, and which actions would be sufficient to heal this divide. After meeting John S. Bennett, the former vice president of the Aspen Institute in Colorado, in 2002 and discovering our shared interest in this problem, we formed a partnership. Later that year we conceived the Cordoba Initiative, naming it after the three-hundred-year period (from the eighth to the eleventh centuries) of the Cordoba caliphate (in what is now Spain) during which Jews, Christians, and Muslims lived in what was then the most enlightened, pluralistic, and tolerant society on earth. We initially designed Cordoba as a multifaith initiative designed to bridge West-Muslim relations by breaking the cycle of mistrust, misunderstanding, and irrational fear that exists between Islam and many parts of the Western world. But partly as a result of being invited to West-Muslim dialogue forums held annually by think tanks across the world, such as the Brookings Institution in Doha, Qatar, and the World Economic Forum in Davos, Switzerland, and by business, political, and human rights groups, it quickly became clear to me that the Cordoba Initiative had to be multinational as well as multifaith.

One result of the Initiative was the Shariah Index Project, under the auspices of which I convened seven meetings of an international cross-section of eminent Muslim legal scholars to define the meaning of the term "Islamic state" from an Islamic legal point of view, and then to measure such "Islamicity" meaningfully—including that of non-Muslim-majority nations. This project would help determine the proper balance in the Muslim world (and elsewhere) between institutions of political power and authority, on the one hand, and institutions of religious power and authority, on the other—the Muslim equivalent of the religion-state relationship. In the United States church-state separation is practically a religious precept all by itself; not so in the Muslim world. The work of this group is a powerful antidote to the perversion of Islam that is currently shaping so much of the political-religious discourse in the Muslim world. It became even more relevant, even essential, after the Arab uprising in 2011, as many Islamic religious parties, such as the

Muslim Brotherhood in Egypt, struggled to help construct new, Islamically faithful democratic countries.

Cordoba House was another of the Initiative's projects; it was designed as a community center and platform to enhance our work and as a multifaith space in the same lower Manhattan neighborhood of Tribeca, about ten blocks south of my mosque on West Broadway. My longer-term interfaith vision, which I had wanted to realize for twenty years, was to establish an Islamic Community Center modeled on the Y's: the YMCA, YWCA, YMHA, and YWHA, originally religious institutions serving their own people without concern for denominational differences, that have become genuine community institutions serving the truly diverse populations in American cities. The remarkable 92nd Street Y, for instance, on New York's Upper East Side, now reaches an extraordinarily diverse range of people with a rich variety of programs, lectures, and concerts, though it was originally intended only for Jews.

When people of different faiths can experience educational programs and basketball leagues and cultural events together, they forge bonds that make harmony possible. I intended Cordoba House to be a "Muslim 92nd Street Y," with a multifaith board and multifaith worship space, including a dedicated Islamic prayer space (a mosque), in a building that architecturally would be thoroughly American, not a transplant from thirteenth-century Cairo. Cordoba House was designed to help build a Muslim community that would be as American as other Muslim communities around the world are Egyptian, Turkish, Iranian, Indian, or Pakistani. And it was to be an American community institution that would be different from any other multifaith organization in the country.

But Cordoba House, now known indelibly, if inaccurately, worldwide as "the Ground Zero mosque," became a flashpoint in 2010 for all of the unhealed wounds of 9/11 and for opportunistic Islamophobes throughout the United States and the world. We faced an onslaught from those who remain financially, politically, and ideologically invested in promoting and sustaining anti-Muslim sentiment. That this effort has aroused such controversy and vitriol demonstrates the size of the task that confronts us if we truly wish to erase our misunderstandings and misconceptions.

It also became a kind of Rorschach test for people everywhere. In our office, we received thousands of letters and emails and phone calls of support from all fifty states and around the world, from Indonesia to Israel. Michael Bloomberg, the Jewish mayor of New York, held a press conference with the Statue of Liberty in the background to proclaim the city's tradition of religious tolerance. New Yorkers held candlelight vigils on our behalf. Speaking to a group of Muslims dining at the White House during Ramadan, the president of the United States defended our right to build Cordoba House "in lower Manhattan in accordance with local laws and ordinances." These expressions confirmed my deep conviction that the great majority of Americans did not want to be at war with Muslims or the Muslim world.

In the middle of this controversy, the leader of a tiny fundamentalist church, the Dove World Outreach Center, in Gainesville, Florida, threatened to burn the Quran on the 2010 anniversary of 9/11. Former Alaska governor Sarah Palin suggested publicly that he should refrain from burning the Quran if we agreed to move Cordoba House. We found ourselves—almost literally—in the midst of a hostage crisis, in which Cordoba House was the hostage. Many Americans considered the Florida pastor ridiculous, but officials at very high levels in the U.S. government worked hard to talk him out of such a politically and religiously inflammatory act.

At the height of the crisis I received a personal letter from the president of Indonesia, Susilo Bambang Yudhoyono, inviting me to give the annual Presidential Lecture that November in Jakarta. He also expressed his deep concern that the Cordoba House project had enflamed Islamophobic sentiments in the United States and supported us in our intention to make the now world-famous "Ground Zero mosque" into a multifaith center. A few weeks later, in his speech to the UN General Assembly in New York, the prime minister of Malaysia, Najib Razak, supported Cordoba House as a multifaith initiative. In that same speech he issued the first call for a global movement of moderates to combat the high-profile extremists who were dominating religious and political debates worldwide.

Had that little congregation in Florida burned the Quran in the middle of the crisis, when emotions were high everywhere, President Yudhoyono told me bluntly at the lecture, it could have been "the beginning of World War III." Three months earlier, during my Gulf nations tour, sponsored by the U.S. State Department, I had met with the crown prince and other leaders of Bahrain, with Sheikha Mozah (the wife of the emir of Qatar), and other leaders of the United Arab Emirates, all of whom were intrigued and alarmed by the "Ground Zero mosque" controversy.

From all of these discussions I learned that the rise of Islamophobia in America is a matter of grave concern to Muslim heads of state. It complicates their ability to have good working relations with the United States. When Americans object to a mosque being built, or spray graffiti on a mosque, or kick Muslims off airplanes, it makes news in the Muslim world. Political opposition (especially Islamic) parties use these images as political fodder against the U.S. government.

Islamophobia also has a disruptive impact on U.S. policy toward the Muslim world. The United States and the Muslim world have critical mutual interests: geopolitical, economic (trade and energy interests), diplomatic, and security (the U.S. military has many bases in the Muslim world, among them naval bases in Bahrain and Qatar). The ever-present danger that we could all be sucked into an endless downward spiral of mistrust and violence demands that Americans—Muslims and non-Muslims alike—take up the task of waging peace in a violent world.

I assured President Yudhoyono that U.S. leaders understood the seriousness of this kind of religious conflict and sought to avoid it. The Bill of Rights, after all, guaranteed Americans genuine religious freedom after more than a thousand years of bloody religious conflict in Europe.

You do not have to be a historian to see that religious wars have never produced the downfall of any religion. The Crusades did not eliminate either Christianity or Islam. Neither did the Hindu-Muslim conflict in India, precipitated by the 1947 division of India into India and Pakistan, defeat either Islam or Hinduism, despite killing half a million people. Nor do I know of a single political regime that took on religion and won. The mighty Roman Empire sought to destroy Christianity by crucifying Christians and throwing them to the lions, yet within three centuries Rome had become the capital of the *Roman* Catholic Church, which continued to grow and thrive for another seventeen centuries. The United States went to war with Mormon Utah in 1857, yet two Republican presidential candidates in 2011 were Mormons. The Nazis tried to eliminate Judaism by committing the worst genocide in modern history, yet Israel was born on the still warm embers of the Third Reich, followed by a renaissance of Jewish culture in the West. And the Soviet Communists tried to do away with all religion, yet today it is Communism itself that has been relegated to history's dustbin, while religion thrives in all the former Soviet republics. There is currently a battle going on between the state and religion in China; which side do you think will win?

The idea that the United States is, or could even consider being, "at war" with Islam, the religion of almost a quarter of the global population, is at once preposterous and profoundly dangerous. In spite of what some American politicians may say for local political gain, I told President Yudhoyono that responsible leaders of both parties understood this fundamental reality. President George W. Bush, for example, paid a public visit to the Islamic Center in Washington right after the 9/11 attacks and emphasized that the United States was battling terrorists, not Islam. Less than five months after assuming office in 2009, President Barack Obama made a point of speaking in Cairo, and just before that in Turkey, emphasizing that America wanted a new and better relationship with the Muslim world. He arrived in Indonesia, where he had lived for a few years as a boy, on November 9, four days after my Presidential Lecture in Jakarta.

Then, a couple of months later, in his 2011 State of the Union address, President Obama uttered a sentence unthinkable for an American president a decade ago: "As extremists try to inspire acts of violence within our borders, we are responding with the strength of our communities, with respect for the rule of law, and with the conviction that American Muslims are part of our American family." He received a spontaneous standing ovation from many members of Congress.

As I listened to the president's address, tears welled up in my eyes. It was not only his words; I was moved by the immediate, spontaneous bipartisan response of the Congress—and the fact that it took place *after* the controversy over Cordoba House had exposed many raw emotions on all sides.

I felt a rush of emotion, convinced that I was watching *the* key turning point for American Muslims, and potentially for the entire complex of relations between the United States and the Muslim world. Truly, as the proverb has it, the night is darkest just before the dawn. U.S.-Muslim relations had bottomed out: the only direction to go from here was up—which is one reason I am so genuinely hopeful about the future.

My Hopes for Muslims and America: Islam the American Way

For too long, and for too many American Muslims, the "hot-button" cultural and religious issues of the day have been swept under the rug by rigid imams, fearful immigrants, and bullying extremists at home and abroad. It is time to deal with all of these issues openly, transparently, and honestly, so that American Muslims see that their religion is not only relevant, but a vital, living guide to the most important, perplexing life-and-death issues in their lives and in the world today.

Islam is an open religion that has embraced new cultures and new realities for 1,400 years. Why would it stop now? In fact, it is orthodox Islam that offers the best arguments to save the Muslim world from the dangers of violent extremism. A genuine understanding of orthodox Islam will undo the misconceptions that Muslims absorb and repeat about their religion all the time—and even foist on others, Muslims and non-Muslims alike.

There is, for example, no Quranic dictum that women must cover their heads or faces as a matter of modesty. There are long-standing differing interpretations of what God means by "modesty" in the Quran. Despite what many Muslims believe—that there is only one "Islamically correct" point of view—it is far more important to respect all legitimate legal opinions, especially when they differ. The Taliban's forcing women to wear the burka was a violation of Islamic law, not its apotheosis.

I see American Muslims—recent immigrants, children of immigrants, and those who have lived here for generations—struggling to integrate themselves into this society while remaining "good Muslims." They fear that they have to satisfy the negative judgments of a God who prohibits and punishes more than He loves and celebrates. But compassion and mercy are not simply words at the beginning of our prayers; this is the way God describes Himself in the beginning of all but one of the Quran's 114 chapters. God states in the Quran (7:156), "I will inflict My punishment upon whom I please; yet My mercy encompasses [is vaster than] everything." The Prophet quotes God as saying "My mercy precedes [overtakes] My wrath" (Bukhari 2954). In another place, the Prophet quotes Him as saying, "O Son of Adam, if your sins reach the heights of heaven and you seek my forgiveness, I will forgive you" (Tirmidhi 2537).

The point is that there is no sin that God does not have the capacity to forgive. And compassion was the practice of God's Messenger, the

Prophet Muhammad, peace and blessings be upon him, as Muslims are wont to say. The Quran (9:128) describes the Prophet as a soul deeply pained by human suffering, ardently solicitous of people's welfare, especially merciful and compassionate.

In the chapters that follow, you will see the God of mercy, justice, and compassion shining through the Quran and in His Prophet Muhammad, in the reports of his sayings and actions known as the *Hadith.* Muslims will see myths common in their mosques turned upside down. You will understand why we Muslims practice Shariah all the time in ways that do not conflict with American law—and that America encourages us to do so, no matter what the state of Oklahoma legislates. You will see the way Islamic law and culture grew out of predecessor pre-Islamic legal traditions, customs, and cultures, and not in isolation. You will understand why for Muslims, Jews and Christians, the People of the Book, as well as adherents of all faiths, are worthy of the deepest religious respect. You will learn about the Prophet's feminism, and that it is cultural conservatives and extremists who have given Islam the image of an antiwoman religion.

Most important of all for the future of America and for the Muslim world, you will see that American Muslims are in the midst of creating a distinctive American Islam of which its practitioners can be proud. Truly, as a popular Muslim saying has it, Islam will rise from the West. And this will be an Islam that is nonviolent, authentic, true to the Quran and the Prophet's teachings, true to its history, spirituality, and legal traditions and continuity of thought, and an Islam that can become globalized. American Islam is a moderate and nonviolent religion, appropriate for a fundamentally moderate country with a political and legal system guaranteeing political freedom, equality, and religious liberty.

The term "Shariah law" has been turned into an epithet and made into a bogeyman that bears little resemblance to a 1,400-year-long tradition of interpretation, legislation, and jurisprudence. The truth is that the United States of America is one of the most "Shariah-compliant" countries on earth. American Muslims are practicing Shariah every time they exercise the religious freedom guaranteed them by the U.S. Constitution. This understanding of Shariah in an American context will help demonstrate the vitality of a moderate understanding of Shariah around the world.

The very fact that the predominantly Christian United States has the largest Jewish population in the world means that American Muslims can live and practice the multifaith relationships envisioned by God and the Prophet more easily than Muslims anywhere else in the world. Here, without being under the pressure of war, dictatorship, or occupation, we can discuss and debate theology and politics with members of other faiths; we can attend one another's worship services; we can even worship together to demonstrate that moderates of all religions have more in common with each other than with the extremists of our individual faiths. The reality of multifaith life in America can truly be a light unto the Muslim world, especially those countries that struggle with religious pluralism.

Islam the American way can easily embrace our faith's gender egalitarianism, which has been considerably more difficult to imagine in some Middle Eastern and North African cultures. Here in the United States a woman served as head of the Islamic Society of North America; there are women presidents of mosques; and soon there will be a theological doctoral program for *muftiyyah*s (women jurists) empowered to issue Islamic legal opinions. American Muslim women are leading the way, not only here in the United States but worldwide, as they have helped devise strategies to wage jihad against violence, combat female genital cutting, fight against domestic violence, and promote women's religious leadership.

Living in one of the crossroads of globalization, American Muslims are grappling with and developing solutions to the dilemmas posed by immigration, including marriage across ethnic, cultural, and religious lines. As open, moderate interpreters of our tradition, American Muslim religious leaders are helping our people find ways through these challenges. The very culture of the United States demands that we do so, unless we simply want to lecture—and lose—our young people.

Conflict between the Muslim world and the West is far from inevitable. I am convinced that human misunderstandings are reparable. No problem created by human beings cannot be solved by human creativity and effort: that's why I'm convinced the relationship can be healed. And in this book I will talk openly about how we can do so, starting with identifying the issues that exist between the Muslim world, broadly conceived, and the West, and then how to solve them. How should we understand extremism and terrorism? What leads to and fuels religious and political extremism, and what can reduce its power and appeal?

Most Muslims abroad *want* to like America, and most Americans *want* to have a better relationship with the Muslim world. That I know from personal experience. The fact that American Muslims are a growing part of the American religious, social, and cultural fabric can help immensely with that process. America itself has the traditions to heal these divisions. Consider the fact that there are now two Muslims in the U.S. House of Representatives. The first, Keith Ellison of Minnesota, took his oath of office on a Quran that had belonged—I love this about America—to none other than Thomas Jefferson. That such a Quran even exists, that it belonged to the architect of the Declaration of Independence, that it was available in the nation's greatest library, that the library lent it to Rep. Ellison for his swearing-in—I am not sure all of these would even be conceivable in any other country on Earth.

I know, from personal experience throughout the Muslim world, that the overwhelming majority of the world's 1.6 billion Muslims disagree profoundly with the extremist, narrow, parochial interpretations of Islam that have gained force in recent decades. Authentic, orthodox, moderate, and nonviolent Islam is a tradition worth rescuing from the extremists.

American Muslims serve in Congress, play professional basketball, sing popular music, report the news, win beauty pageants, drive cabs, serve in the military, go to college, teach school, heal the sick, and build buildings. Our food, our faith, and our values are enriching American culture, and because our numbers are growing, there is much more to come. American Muslims are helping lead the way toward reclaiming their religion, playing an essential role in creating a more tolerant and just twenty-first-century America—and world.

1
WHAT WE BELIEVE

Witnessing God: The Commandments of Our Faith

I grew up mostly in Malaysia, a Muslim-majority country, the eldest son of a well-known Muslim scholar and imam. As a boy I prayed, like other Muslims, five times a day. At the core of these prayers we recite, in Arabic, what is known as the *shahada,* or "witness of faith," a ritual declaration that translates as "I bear witness that there is no god but God and I bear witness that Muhammad is God's Messenger."

When I was twelve or thirteen I had a problem with the *shahada*: every time I recited it I heard a voice inside me saying, "Feisal, you're a hypocrite. In your prayers you are saying that you bear witness to God, when the truth is that you haven't witnessed God at all; you are simply mouthing the words." Teenagers are highly sensitive to what they believe to be hypocrisy in others, so it was excruciating to hear this voice accusing *me,* especially when I knew it was telling the truth. I knew little about my faith at the time, but I would later learn that the Quran is filled with God's criticism of hypocrisy and hypocrites.

One day, during our midday meal—it was our main meal of the day—I put my problem to my father. "Doesn't the word *shahada* mean 'to bear witness,' that is, 'to see'?" "Yes, Feisal," he replied. I continued, "And doesn't *ash-hadu an la ilaha illallah* therefore mean 'I have seen, or witnessed, that there is no god but God'?" "Yes, Feisal," he again answered. "But I haven't seen God yet," I all but wailed, and waited for a rebuke. My dad did not look surprised or angry or even annoyed—and he did not, thank goodness, think me a hypocrite. He was a great teacher and a wise man, so he understood the significance of what I was seeking: that inner moment of experience or enlightenment, what Sufis (Muslims who seek this experience of God) call "the unveiling" of God.

While suggesting that I simply continue with my prayers, he also guided me to writings that he thought would be helpful in my quest. He had a friend at the university who taught Sufism, whom I visited and who pointed me toward books that attempt to help the individual achieve spiritual realization, to recognize God. I read and read, especially the writings of Imam Ghazali, the great eleventh- and twelfth-century Sufi philosopher, which I found particularly inspiring. And I prayed and prayed, and pleaded with God to hear my prayers.

I got an important part of the answer when I read a story by the thirteenth-century poet Rumi, called "Two Friends." A man goes to a friend's house and knocks loudly, imperiously, on the door. From within, a voice asks, "Who's there?" to which the man answers, "It is I." The voice retorts, "Go away." Disappointed, he leaves. After a year of wandering and spiritual reflection, the man comes back, this time humbly and with a trembling heart, and knocks on the door with trepidation. The voice inside asks again, "Who's there?" This time the man answers, "It is you." The friend says, "Please come in, my self, there's no place in this house for two."

One afternoon about a year after that first conversation with my father, I was riding home from school on the bus and suddenly, out of nowhere, it happened. For what seemed like a long minute, though I don't know how long it actually lasted, I could feel my own personal boundaries dissolve. Without losing consciousness—in fact, I was extremely aware of everything around me—the boundaries of my own self, my ego, just melted away, and in that moment I felt a complete oneness with everything around me, and oneness with God. At that moment I *knew* directly, experientially, with no shadow of a doubt, that I was in the presence of a being absolutely almighty, all-knowing, all-loving, merciful, and compassionate, who comprehended everything in existence. And I knew that everything was perfect, that the universe was the way it should be.

To this day I remember that moment vividly. I remember the greenness of the leaves and the bus driving me home, the yellow of the afternoon sun, the grinding of the bus's diesel engine, even the rip in the brown vinyl seat to my left. And I felt at one with all of it: with God, with the sounds, with the colors, with the feelings and sensations. We all were one. When the moment was over, I knew that I had borne witness to God. As in Rumi's story, I felt that God had finally invited me in—and I was now a genuine witness to God. Sufis have a saying: *Once the heart prostrates itself before God, it never rises, remaining eternally in prostration.* With this initial experience of God's reality, I felt I had performed this prostration, an act so transformative that I saw everything in a new light. And that feeling has never left me. It has enabled me to practice my religion authentically, from the inside out, instead of experiencing the forced practice of religion from the outside in, which results in strained and often fake religiosity.

The First Commandment: Bearing Witness to the Oneness of God

Islam is a faith based on the Quran, a collection of God's words revealed to the Prophet Muhammad through the Angel Jibril (whom Christians know as the Angel Gabriel) between 610 and 632, when the Prophet died, and the practice, or *sunna,* of the Prophet as described in the collected reports, or *Hadith,* of his teachings and practice. In the nearly 1,400 years since the Prophet's death, an immense body of commentary has emerged to explain, interpret, and elaborate the meaning of the Quran, the Prophet's actions, and the *Hadith,* which, depending on the tradition, number into the hundreds of thousands. Nevertheless the religion practiced by Muslims in America and around the world is also one of breathtaking simplicity.

Most fundamentally of all, we believe there is just one God, whom we love and worship above all else. Like Christianity and Judaism, Islam was born in an era of polytheism, a time when Greeks, Romans, Babylonians, and tribes and kingdoms worshipped many gods, often through idols. We Muslims acknowledge, affirm, declare, and worship one God. This God, our God, has no partners. The Lord is one. Our single most important act of worship is to declare the following: "There is no god but God." In Arabic: *La ilaha illallah.*

If you are not Muslim, you might try saying it, as we do, several times in a row, just as it is written. The front of the tongue goes to the roof of the mouth to make the "l" sound. Not only is it a profound declaration of monotheism; it has an alliterative rhythm (repeating the "la" sound) that helps move it into the realm of Arabic poetry, which makes much use of alliteration.

Among Sufis, repeating this phrase is the basis of all meditative practice, known as *dhikr,* similar to a Buddhist *mantra. Dhikr* means "remembrance (of God)," which in turn elicits God's remembrance of us, as God commands us, "Remember Me so I will remember you" (Quran 2:152). God often commands us in the Quran to remember Him. One of the Prophet's companions complained he was too old to perform all five of the daily prayers, and he asked the Prophet to give him something easier to do. "Occupy your tongue with the mention of Allah," the Prophet answered (Tirmidhi 1970). As important as the five-times-daily prayer is, the Prophet did not rebuke the old man, but urged him to frequently remember God, for the Quran (29:45) asserts that remembrance of God is greater than prayer.

It is greater because that is how we connect with God, the spiritual source that enlightens and transforms us into loving creatures. It is greater because connecting with God is how we internally realize and experience the underlying unity of all faiths and experientially connect with adherents of all faiths. To use a business metaphor, we have a tendency to think of Judaism as resembling "Moses, Inc.," Christianity as "Jesus, Inc.," and Islam as "Muhammad, Inc." The Quranic truth is that Moses, Jesus, Muhammad, and all the countless prophets God sent were regional managers of "God, Inc." Divine remembrance transforms us from religious observers who are attached to Judaism, Christianity, and Islam as crystallizations of Moses, Inc., Jesus, Inc., and Muhammad, Inc., into adherents of God, Inc., and seeing Moses, Jesus, Muhammad, and all the prophets as crystallizations of God, Inc., in different contexts of time and place. Divine remembrance is the source of spiritual power and the enlivening power behind nonviolence.

The Prophet bid his followers repeat *La ilaha illallah* as often as they could, and to this day Muslims are encouraged to repeat it frequently, to the point that it is constantly on our tongues. Depending on context and how it is intoned, the words *Allah* and *La ilaha illallah* can be exclaimed by Muslims to mean any number of things (just as Americans use the exclamations "Good God!" or "God Almighty!" to indicate surprise or wonder). But the repetition, a hundred or even a thousand times a day, to fill up dead time, to express thankfulness for good fortune, for the beauty of the day, for the love of one's family, is considered a very beneficial and potentially transformative practice. It can even be a kind of stress reducer. I know someone who looks forward to a traffic jam so she can repeat *La ilaha illallah*!

Islam is not alone in this exercise of expressing the oneness of God. If you are Jewish, you may hear the echoes of the Hebrew *Shema,* "Hear O Israel, the Lord our God, the Lord is One" (in Hebrew, *Shema Yisrael, Adonai Elohenu, Adonai Echad,* which sounds strikingly similar to the first verse of chapter 112 of the Quran: *qul huwa-llahu ahad,* meaning "Say, He is God: One") and the following instruction, part of the *Shema,* known in Hebrew as the *v'ahavta*:

> You shall love the Lord your God with all your heart, and with all your soul, and with all your might. Keep these words that I am

> commanding you today in your heart. Recite them to your children and talk about them when you are at home and when you are away, when you lie down and when you rise. Bind them as a sign on your hand, fix them as an emblem on your forehead, and write them on the doorposts of your house and on your gates. (Deuteronomy 6:5–9)

Jews often place a *mezuzah,* a decorative case holding small scraps of paper imprinted with Torah verses, on their doorframes. Muslims do something similar: the expression *La ilaha illallah* is often written in beautiful calligraphy and posted on entrances to people's homes, and today it even appears on bumper stickers and digitally on laptops.

If you are Christian, you may be reminded of Matthew 22:37–38, in which Jesus quotes the Torah: "'You shall love the Lord your God with all your heart, and with all your soul, and with all your mind.' This is the greatest and first commandment." These similarities are no accident, of course. Muslims believe that the Torah and the Gospels were also divine revelation from the same almighty God, and believe in Moses and Jesus as our prophets too.

The First Commandment of Islam, then, is to bear witness to the oneness of God. We incorporate the *La ilaha illallah* into the full *shahada,* which is this statement: "I bear witness that there is no god but God and I bear witness that Muhammad is God's messenger." By making this statement, we are bearing witness to God's oneness, God's power, and God's revelations to the Prophet (and thereby to all the prophets), which are collected in the Quran. It is a covenantal act, an active commitment rather than an article of passive belief.

This commandment is the foundation of our faith and the key to our religion, the group of beliefs, practices, and obligations defining the relationship between the individual and God. It is the defining pillar of Islam. To me, it is the defining pillar of religion itself.

Here is what I mean, and why I give so much importance to the First Commandment. The Quran, while acknowledging Jews and Christians, never once speaks of Judaism or Christianity. God never once addresses the Prophet's followers as "Muslims" in the Quran. He always calls them "believers" (*mu'mins*). In the Quran (9:29, 9:23), God talks about believers, about "right" or "good" religion (*din al-haq* and *din al-qayyimah*), and "God's religion" (*din Allah*), and asserts that each of the prophets and messengers came to teach the same religion in a different time, in different languages, and with slightly different liturgical practices.

The Prophet himself always referred to his community as "believers." The caliphs appointed as leaders of the community after the Prophet's death were known as "Commanders of the Believers," not "Commanders of the Muslims," and did in fact rule over a growing multifaith community. Only a century later did we change our name from "believers" to "Muslims." This change occurred because the Prophet's followers felt the need to differentiate themselves from other faith communities, especially the Jews and Christians, who were also considered believers, literally "People of the Book" (people who were given a Scripture: in the Jews' case the Torah and the Psalms; in the Christians' case, the Gospels).

We all, Jews and Christians and Muslims alike, have a tendency to (in effect) "worship" our own religion and our own religious laws and practices and articles of faith, when the core of each of our religions really ought to be the First Commandment: the acknowledgment of and bearing witness to the greatness and oneness of God. The Prophet instructed his followers *not* to worship him, but to worship God. The Hebrew prophets make this precise criticism of the Children of Israel, and Jesus does something very similar. This criticism and commandment are just as relevant today, in the religiously diverse United States—and the world—where far too many believers are more attached to their denominational understandings of rituals and doctrinal niceties than they are to the genuine basis of their belief.

I almost wish we could use the ancient language and call ourselves "believers" rather than Muslims. In our zeal to exalt our own religions, we lose sight of what we have in common, which is deeper than any particular manifestation of a religious faith. More than once in the Quran (6:159, 30:32) God laments our human predilection to divide ourselves into sects, each delighting and congratulating itself on its limited understanding of "true faith" and looking down its nose at others.

If all of us, including today's Muslims, were to return to thinking of ourselves as believers in this larger sense, it would expand the space for more interfaith interaction and mutual respect among those who consider themselves believers. We would be closer to what the Prophet was trying to create in Medina, a community of believers that included his followers and some who believed in God through the path of Jesus, others through the path of Moses.

This language would, I believe, create a sense of a believing community that could also cross national and ethnic boundaries. This is why, in the early history of Islam, there was recognition and protection of other faith communities and aiding them in being the best possible Jews and Christians. Followers of the Prophet thought of themselves as believers building communities of faith, rather than thinking of themselves in a parochial sense as Muslims in contrast to Christians or Jews. They did not exclude those outside their faith as being outside their community and did not believe they had to have a hostile relationship with them. Instead of focusing on defining "the other," the concept of believers expands the notion of "us."

If you think about this idea, you can see that it offers a way back from the extraordinary religious divisions and conflicts of our time: expanding the notion of "us" rather than establishing differences between "us" and "them" as a cause of enmity. Because once we start down the path of defining and rigidifying differences, the space of "our community" shrinks: one group of Sunni Muslims, for example, begins to regard every other group, including the Shias, as heretics and enemies. The same phenomenon has occurred, especially among Christians over the centuries, in literal battles between Protestants and Catholics, but also within Jewish communities.

The "Islamic" Word: Expressing a Theology

There is a tripartite model in Islamic theology, based on one of the most important *hadith*s, known as the *hadith* of Jibril (or Gabriel), organized around three concepts: *islam,* or submission; *iman,* or faith, and *ihsan,* or virtue (Muslim 1). The translations are not exact, but they will do for our purposes.

Islam, I want to emphasize, is understood to be the lowest level of religious adherence, even though it consists of the "five pillars" of religious practice that all *Muslims* (those who submit) must perform as obligations. These practices unite Muslims from Los Angeles to Lahore, Detroit to Dar es Salaam. At this most basic level, the Prophet defined the term "Islam" as a set of *actions,* things that we do, not a *concept* in which we believe. It is God we primarily have to believe in, and not Islam. It is not enough, in other words, to know that God exists; we must also bear witness to Him.

In the past few centuries, the term "Islam" has evolved from a verbal noun to a proper noun, as a religion we belong to rather than the set of actions we perform. We have created the adjective "Islamic" to describe things that would have puzzled our Arabic-speaking ancestors. These words only make sense because we are looking at ourselves from the point of view of outsiders, using a modern terminology that is alien to our tradition.

A confident, righteous people doesn't define itself from others' point of view. We ought to be defining ourselves based on our own sense of selfhood and our own relationship to God, not in the fuzzy language of being "Islamic" or "un-Islamic." People or cultures or nations are either godly or ungodly, abiding by God's laws, surrendering to Him and obeying His laws, or not. But since the advent of colonialism, too many Muslims have fallen in love with the term "Islamic" and have sought to "Islamize" everything; thus we have "Islamic state," "Islamic banking," "Islamic dress," "Islamic food," "Islamic Barbie," and the like. Is it any wonder, then, that non-Muslims also extend the Islamization process to include "Islamic bomb" and "Islamic terrorism"? Although these terms are genuinely offensive and frequently nonsensical to Muslims, we have been partly responsible for their creation. Unless we take responsibility for this usage and seek to erase it, I believe we cannot in good conscience completely place the blame for this usage on non-Muslims.

Even some of the best interpreters of the Muslim world make what seems to me a fundamental error when they use the word "Islam" to refer to the entire history and belief systems of Muslims and the Muslim world. It is a profound mistake to think of individuals or Muslim groups as identical to Islam the faith, just as it is an error to consider individual or groups of Christians as identical to Christianity. This way of thinking results in people asking, "Why does Islam do this?" or "What does Islam think about this?"

Nomenclature is critical here. Islam is the five actions believers are required to perform. It is not really a proper noun; it's a verb form, a gerund, like "surrendering." In Arabic, you never ask, "What does Islam say?" The proper and classical way of phrasing this question is "What does God say?" or "What did the Prophet say?" or "What do the majority of scholars say?" When the questions are phrased in this manner the answer must naturally take note that God has said different things in different contexts, that the Prophet gave different judgments in different contexts and at different stages of his community's evolution. It is God who commands, and God commands *islam*. Islam does not command!

If you ask, on the other hand, "What does Islam say?" you have transformed "Islam" into a proper noun, into an actor in its own right, and incorporated the implicit presumption that there is one answer and anything else is "un-Islamic" and heretical. You collapse the diversity of opinion and law, which has been a part of the robustness and health of living societies over centuries. The question itself is structurally wrong, historically invalid, and logically false.

The same is true of the question "What does America think?" If

"America" thinks something, then all Americans—Tea Partiers and teachers' union shop stewards, environmentalists and oil company CEOs, politicians and plumbers—think exactly the same thing, which we know to be false. But if we shoehorn all Americans into one set of "correct beliefs" on a whole set of issues, from dress to politics to what is healthy food to whether abortion should be legal or illegal, then every opposing view will be de facto "un-American." Now you get the idea of what has happened to Muslims over the past half-century. If journalists and public officials speak of "Islam," they collapse the experience and history of more than a billion people over a millennium and a half into one category of interpretation.

Now that I have gotten this pet peeve out of the way, let us return to *islam,* the five action-obligations. First is to make the declaration of the *shahada:* "I bear witness that there is no god but God and I bear witness that Muhammad is God's Messenger." (That alone, by the way, declared publicly, is required for embracing Islam and will gain you formal entrance into the Muslim community as a convert.) Second, we ritually pray to God while facing Mecca five times a day: at dawn, noon, midafternoon, sunset, and early night. These prayers are prescribed, memorized by all Muslims, and involve a certain choreography (standing, bowing, prostrating, and sitting in a particular order) that is pretty much identical across the world. I say "pretty much" because there are some very slight differences between Sunnis and Shias on this choreography. But Sunnis and Shias may, and do, pray together, and such prayers are all deemed valid. Because we believe that God dictated the Quran to the Prophet in Arabic, this Muslim liturgical prayer is performed exclusively in Arabic, the way the Mass used to be entirely in Latin and Jewish services all in Hebrew.

The narrative of how the prayer began is the subject of a story in the *Hadith* (Bukhari 3596). One day, while the Prophet was asleep in Mecca, the Archangel Jibril put him on a winged horse that flew him to the site of the destroyed Temple of Solomon in Jerusalem—

now occupied by the Dome of the Rock. After praying there with all the prophets, he was raised through the seven heavens, where he met and conversed with various prophets (including Adam, Abraham, and Jesus) and witnessed many things. Among the sights he witnessed was angels adoring God and singing His praises. At one level of heaven he witnessed infinite rows of angels eternally worshipping God in a standing position; as he ascended to the next level he saw angels in a bowing position, at the next level angels in a prostrate position, at the next level in a seated position. The Prophet was so moved by this powerful image of rows and rows of angels singing and glorifying God that God established it as the choreography of the prayer movements for his followers.

Muslims are also known around the world for our call to prayer, chanted by muezzins five times daily in mosques. The origin of the call to prayer, itself now something of an art form, also makes a good story. When the Prophet emigrated from Mecca and established the first community of believers in Medina, he built a mosque. The question soon arose: how to call the believers to assemble for prayer in the mosque in such a way as not to be confused with Jews' use of the ram's horn, the *shofar,* or the bell that Christians used.

At first, they decided to use a gong, but then one day one of the Prophet's companions reported that he had had a dream in which he heard these words as a call to prayer: "God is the greatest. I bear witness that there is no god but God. I bear witness that Muhammad is God's Messenger. Come to prayer. Come to success. God is the greatest. There is no god but God." The Prophet announced that this dream was a sign from God (Abu Dawud 421). He instructed his community that a call to prayer would be recited out loud in place of a gong. Then he asked his friend, the freed Ethiopian slave Bilal, who had a fine voice, to climb to the roof of the mosque and chant the words publicly. The very first time the people of Medina heard this call, the beauty of his rendition echoing off the alleyways of the city stopped them in their tracks, holding the Prophet and his followers in a kind of awe. This chant has been the Muslim call to prayer ever since. It is such a powerful and beautiful chant that muezzins compete over who can produce the finest rendition.

The third action-obligation central to Islam is to donate, annually, at least 2.5 percent of our wealth, called the *zakat,* both to support the needy and to benefit the larger community. In some Muslim-majority countries (Saudi Arabia, Pakistan, Malaysia), the *zakat* is collected by the state-run *zakat* treasuries, who then distribute them; in other countries, it is entirely voluntary and distributed directly to the needy. In the United States Muslims give the *zakat* to their mosques, relief organizations, or other favorite charities.

Fourth, we are enjoined to fast—to refrain from eating, drinking, and sexual activity—from dawn to sunset during the month of Ramadan.

Because of their different interpretations of God's words in the Quran, Sunnis and Shias end their fasts differently. I experienced an amusing example of this difference when I was invited some years ago to the home of the Iranian ambassador to the United Nations in New York during Ramadan. He had invited American Muslim leaders from all over the United States for this meal; most of them were Shia. Sunset came and went, and people kept talking, and I found myself increasingly confused. We Sunnis rush to break our fast at the very instant of sunset, and I was hungry for the delicious *fesenjan, tadik,* and other Iranian delicacies! After fifteen minutes or so, I leaned over to one of the Shia imams and gently whispered that sunset had passed. "Oh," he explained, "we don't break our fast at sunset, we wait until the onset of first night in the East, about twenty to thirty minutes after sunset, in keeping with the Quranic verse 'to complete the fast until night'" (Quran 2:187). Shias don't interpret "night" as sunset the way Sunnis do. This made perfect sense, I thought, though I had never heard this interpretation before. You will have deduced from this story that I am Sunni, and that I did not spend much time with Shias in my early life.

Fifth, we are to make a pilgrimage to Mecca (known as the *hajj*), assuming we are physically and financially able, at least once in our lifetime.

These ritual acts connect Muslims to each other all over the world, in ways that are often quite moving. For example, Malcolm X's letter to his friends and family from his own *hajj* (reprinted in his *Autobiography*) is one of the true highlights of American religious writing:

> Never have I witnessed such sincere hospitality and the overwhelming spirit of true brotherhood as is practiced by people of all colors and races here in this Ancient Holy Land, the home of Abraham, Muhammad, and all the other prophets of the Holy Scriptures. For the past week, I have been utterly speechless and spellbound by the graciousness I see displayed all around me by people of all colors . . . from blue-eyed blonds to black-skinned Africans. But we were all participating in the same ritual, displaying a spirit of unity and brotherhood that my experiences in America had led me to believe never could exist between the white and the non-white.

Although they are called the five "pillars of the faith," acts through which we submit ourselves to almighty God, the truth is that we can perform these movements and actions without really believing in them, without having a sense of deep faith, without ever having truly witnessed God. In the Quran, for instance, God explicitly recognizes that a person can be a Muslim—someone outwardly performing the actions—and be spiritually empty. Or worse. A person can be intentionally hypocritical and unethical—a wolf, so to speak, in sheep's clothing (Quran 2:264).

In the Quran (3:113–115) we read that there are Jews and Christians who are sincere and devout, who compete in acts of goodness, and who will receive God's approval and salvation. So there are upright people of faith of whom God approves, whether they call themselves Christians or Jews or believers or Muslims, and there are hypocrites and evildoers in all these religious categories as well. The real divide is therefore not between Muslims, Jews, Christians, and Buddhists, but between godly believers and ungodly people—which includes religious hypocrites. We must work to make the godly/ungodly divide dominate over the current attempts to divide Muslims against Jews and Christians and Hindus.

Anyone can perform these actions for show rather than belief and can be unethical or cruel in dealings with others; in either case the person would be engaging in hypocrisy, one of the most serious sins discussed in the Quran, with an entire chapter devoted to it (chapter 63). Another chapter condemns those "who perform the prayers, but who are forgetful of their prayers" (that is, do not act accordingly: Quran 107:4–5).

Calling ourselves *Muslims,* therefore, in this theological and historical sense, ought not by itself to be a great source of pride. After all, in Quranic terms Muslims are in effect probationary believers, a full step below where we need to be: real believers (people of *iman,* belief or faith), which is the next step up in this system. Believers are called to five core "items of faith": belief in one God, the supreme being; belief in angels (such as Gabriel, Azrael, and Michael); belief in the Holy Scriptures of Jews and Christians—the Torah, the Psalms, and the Gospels—as well as the Quran as originally and fully God's compositions; belief in the prophets and messengers of God; and belief in the Last Day (a complex of events, including the end of the world, a day of resurrection followed by a day of divine judgment, followed by eternal reward in Paradise or punishment in Hell). There is no tradition of doctrinal dispute or cherry-picking among these beliefs in Islam, the way some Christians will argue about the virgin birth or the resurrection or the literal existence of heaven and hell. For us, this is a complete package comprising core beliefs.

As you can see, belief goes a step further than practice. If we truly believe the words of the Holy Scriptures, we cannot simply go through the motions of prayer or financial charity. We have to practice in our daily lives what God instructs: to free ourselves of hypocrisy, egoism, and self-delusion and to seek justice for our community.

There is an ancient argument among believers that is as old as religion and has manifested itself in theological debates and creedal competitions over the centuries. It has to do with whether salvation depends on faith alone, by God's grace, without "works"—actions in society—or whether salvation might come to those who may not have true faith but who perform good works. God frequently commands us in the Quran "Believe and do good works" (Quran 2:62) and also "Establish prayer and pay the *zakat*" (Quran 2:110). So it is clear to me that we need both faith *and* good works, prayer *and* charity, to win God's grace and approval.

If this sounds as though I am calling for a kind of revival here in the United States in the early twenty-first century, you are reading me correctly. I am calling for the same kind of return to spirituality that Jesus called for in his lifetime. Jesus criticized the emphasis on religious legalism that allowed money changers into the Temple of God. As he violated the letter of Sabbath laws, he declared, "The Sabbath was made for humankind, and not humankind for the Sabbath" (Mark 2:27). Many Muslims, especially those who are influencing our young, are concerned only with legalities and have dispensed with the spirit of the law. I would like to see a return to our original tradition of calling ourselves *believers,* not merely *Muslims,* and demanding of our community a serious level of faith commitment and ethical virtue.

We contrast this level with what we call *ihsan,* often translated as "virtue," which the Prophet described as "worshipping God as if you see Him." This highest level is the one closest to God, and one few of us think we can actually reach. But since the concept is based in the word for "doing that which is the good, or the better or best" it suggests a constant effort to become more virtuous, to see God more clearly, to become closer to God. Experiencing God makes a person more virtuous. You can see how much of the Prophet's teachings are rooted in action: active practice, active belief, and the struggle to achieve the best and thereby actually do better.

We all tend to act more responsibly and ethically when we know we are being watched than when we are alone. God is watching us all the time, and we human beings need to act with that knowledge.

You can see how this highest level, *ihsan,* links back to the *shahada,* since the act of witnessing necessarily implies that one sees God. To witness something, after all, is to see and be present to it. So to worship as if you can see God requires us to perform the *shahada* as something real. That was my problem as a boy: I did not feel it was real, and until it was real, it tormented me.

When I tell the story from my childhood of how I came to internalize God, I get powerful reactions from different kinds of people. No matter the audience, both Muslims and non-Muslims respond strongly. The search for God is universal. If there is a God, how do we *really* know He exists? How *can* we know? These questions are not unique to any one religious community. Religion begins with spirituality, the experience of God that binds all people of faith. People are touched by the idea that Muslims and Christians and Jews share a powerful hunger for experiencing the presence of God, what American Christians used to call a "conversion" and Buddhists "enlightenment."

The Second Commandment: Love Others as Ourselves

My personal experience of God on that school bus had a profound impact on my relationship with Him: how I prayed and worshipped, how I threw myself into deeper readings on religion and religious philosophy, my experience of fasting, my desire to go on the *hajj*. All of these actions became more intense, more consequential to me. But it also deeply affected how I related to others and made me so much more eager to understand how God wanted me to relate to my world: to my parents, family, friends, teachers, and strangers, but also to animals and the rest of the natural environment. For when I experienced God, I simultaneously perceived Him in His handiwork, so to speak: in the mountains, in the sky, in the colors of a sunrise or sunset, in the dogs and cats and other animals around us, in all of nature. I felt friendly, even intimate toward nature, for which I felt grateful to God. And I wanted to relate differently, better to the Creator of all this beauty. I desperately wanted to earn God's approval, and the possibility that I might evoke His displeasure made me feel horrible.

Which brings us to the Second Commandment of Islam, equal in importance to the First. It will be familiar to Jews and Christians (and all other religious communities), as was the First Commandment. Most simply, it is the Golden Rule: to love our neighbors as ourselves. In the words of the Prophet, "None of you is a believer until you love for your brother what you love for yourself" (Bukhari 12). The Prophet's Farewell Sermon commands, "Hurt no-one, so that no-one may hurt you" (Muslim 2129). Or, as the Jewish teacher Hillel answered when dared to summarize the Torah while the challenger stood on one foot, "What is hateful to you do not do unto your fellow human being; this is the whole of the Torah; the rest is commentary; go and learn." Not an easy task.

Preventing people from doing what is hateful to others is what God's law is all about, and this is why I will now discuss law.

2

SHARIAH IN AMERICA

Fathoming the Second Commandment

In 1995 my studies and understanding of Islam took a new turn. Daisy's uncle invited me to speak to the Islamic Medical Association conference that year on "the Islamic viewpoint" regarding some thorny dilemmas in medical ethics that he and other Muslim doctors were struggling with. Their aim was to develop a problem-solving format that would help Muslim physicians think through such issues as abortion, surrogate motherhood, and termination of life support in such a way that their decisions would be consistent with Muslim principles. I knew that the basis of Islamic law flows from our understanding of how to apply the Second Commandment: the dos and don'ts of how to treat others. But I realized that in order to be helpful to the Medical Association I needed to know much more about how to apply the systematic philosophy or science of Islamic law, known as *fiqh al-shariah,* literally the "understanding of God's ordinances."

I did quite a lot of reading and research and developed a template for understanding which issues belong to the jurist and which to the medical professional, even though many of these issues, such as end-of-life decisions, are in fact blended concerns. The doctors were appreciative and wanted also to see the research notes I had taken. The notes were a mess, so I began to put them together in a format the doctors could use. In doing so I discovered that the issues were so complex and important that I found myself writing more and more, until I ended up writing an entire book on Islamic law. I also found that there was so much ignorance and misinformation floating around regarding Shariah, even among Muslims, that I subtitled the book *What Every Muslim Should Know About the Shariah.*

As is the case with other major religions based in divinely given scriptures, writings that predate the industrial age, Islamic law has to deal with developments—scientific, technological, political, and social—undreamed of centuries or millennia earlier. U.S. constitutional law and American courts have struggled with many of the same issues; highly publicized cases on abortion or when to end life support for terminally ill or failing patients prove how contentious such issues can be. Neither the framers nor classical Shariah scholars envisioned electronic communication, medical respirators, nanotechnology, or the Internet.

Today such decisions in the Muslim world are made by committees that comprise legal scholars and subject area experts (medical doctors in the case of medical questions, economic experts in questions pertaining to finance). Many regard their collective wisdom in achieving consensus as the legally valid approach to determining a way through these issues. In one such decision, brain death has been widely accepted as the Shariah definition of when a person is dead, thereby enabling doctors and loved ones to "pull the plug" with God's blessing.

When the U.S. Supreme Court was debating the *Roe v. Wade* case in 1973, my father was asked to submit a legal brief on the Shariah position on abortion. While his own position was that abortion was justified only if the life of the mother was threatened, his sense of academic and legal professionalism required that he provide an analysis of the positions of the different schools of law, including that of the Shafii school, which applies the *hadith* saying that the human soul enters the fetus at 120 days, and that therefore human life begins at 120 days. I have often wondered if the Supreme Court used that opinion in its decision making abortion legal on demand during the first trimester. Since people all over the world have very different opinions on such medical and personal issues, I have to continuously remind them that different schools provide different interpretations of the law.

If instead of a movement to pass laws against Shariah, we had an open and thoughtful exchange between Shariah scholars and American legal scholars and judges, such a dialogue could be of enormous value, not only in integrating Muslims in America, but in helping Muslims to interpret Shariah in the modern Western context. Then American Muslims could have an even greater impact on the world Muslim community.

What Does God Want of Me?

That the Second Commandment, in combination with the First, is the basis of all law was said best by Jesus. A Pharisee, an expert in the law, tried to trap him with this question:

> "Teacher, which commandment in the law is the greatest?" He said to him, "'You shall love the Lord your God with all your heart, and with all your soul, and with all your mind.'" This is the greatest and first commandment. And a second is like it: "You shall love your neighbor as yourself." On these two commandments hang all the law and the prophets. (Matthew 22:36–40)

"On these two commandments hang all the law and the prophets." These two commandments, the foundation of Judaism and the bedrock of Christianity, are likewise the core of Muslim faith and Muslim understanding of God's Law, on which all else is built. To me "all the law and the prophets" that Jesus spoke of naturally included the Prophet Muhammad and God's Law as revealed to him, a belief that was corroborated by the Quran in verse 42:13, where God says, "He has ordained [*shara'a*] for you as law [*din,* a word also translated as "religion"], that which He enjoined upon Noah, and that which We revealed to you, and which We enjoined upon Abraham, Moses and Jesus."

This is why the Prophet, and the scholars and judges who followed him, saw themselves as following in a continuous legal tradition from Jewish and Christian law and Abrahamic law, which was presumably the law and custom of the Arabs before the time of the Prophet. When the Prophet fled Mecca and established the community of believers in Medina, part of the penal code he established there was based on biblical law, until God made specific revelations in the Quran that modified biblical law. Later revelations always modify what came before, generally because of new contexts. According to Christians, Jesus brought a new understanding of the Sabbath. For Muslims, God revised some features of biblical law and religious observance, and adapted them to seventh-century Arabian society.

God's Law as commanded by the Quran and the Prophet is the lens through which we Muslims learn how to think about and differentiate between right and wrong behavior: what is ethical or unethical behavior, legitimate or illegitimate governance, appropriate civil and criminal punishments, and protection of human rights.

The Arabic word for God's laws, His list of do's and don'ts, is *shar',* which means "ordinances," a term that evolved into the word *Shariah,* the single word that scares non-Muslims more than any other, confuses millions of faithful Muslims, and even pits many against each other violently.

Shariah, or Shariah law, as English speakers commonly call it, conjures up images in American minds of the Taliban stoning adulterers in stadiums or of the Iranian morals police arresting women for inappropriate dress. Why else would dozens of American states consider outlawing Shariah within their borders? Muslims know, deep down, that this is a deeply distorted picture of an integral part of our faith.

For Muslims, wherever they live, Shariah means the law decreed by

God in the Quran, through the Prophet—for whatever the Prophet commanded separately from the Quran has God's sanction as well—and as understood and elaborated by Muslim legal scholars over the past fourteen centuries. Since the root of the word lies in the word meaning "to ordain," in the sense of "to command," we understand Shariah as "God's commandments" or "God's legislation." Shariah includes all of God's ordinances and commandments: prescriptions and prohibitions. As a result, it also reaches back to the Torah and the biblical Ten Commandments, which all Abrahamic faiths share.

But most precisely and technically, Shariah consists of the roughly 150 to 500 Quranic verses that prescribe or prohibit behavior, called *ayat al-ahkam,* and the roughly 1,200 to 1,500 *hadith*s of the Prophet that also command or prohibit, called *ahadith al-ahkam.* (The difference in number is a function of the school of jurisprudence.) They constitute the basis of all Islamic law. (The origin of Jewish law, *Halacha,* though it predates Shariah, also lies in a body of divine ordinances, the 613 *mitzvot,* or commandments in the Torah: 365 prescriptions and 248 prohibitions.)

The best way for Americans to understand the relationship between the Quran and Shariah is to think of the U.S. Constitution and the Declaration of Independence, the legal foundation of all American law. (The Constitution, of course, unlike the Quran, is an entirely secular document that avoids discussion of spiritual matters. It is the structural relationship between the Constitution and American law that I am interested in here.) All the subsequent laws enacted by Congress over the past 200 years, decisions of all the federal and state courts, all decisions by county and municipal judges—all have to be constitutional in the sense that they must not contradict the Constitution. If Congress or a state legislature enacts a law that violates the Constitution, courts can strike it down. For Muslims, the 500 Quranic verses and 1,200 prophetic commandments that we call Shariah play a role similar to that played by the Constitution for Americans versus state laws.

In addition to the opinions of judges and justices, American legal scholars have written voluminously on how to understand and interpret the Constitution and the framers' intent. They have developed methodologies and philosophies of the law, in part based on Supreme Court decisions; this body of scholarship is called jurisprudence.

Muslim scholars divided the law into two parts: all the laws pertaining to worship and belief (*'ibadat*), which are First Commandment laws, and all those pertaining to worldly affairs (*mu'amalat*), which are Second Commandment laws. The basic structure of Islamic law, in other words, which is built upon these two commandments, follows Jesus' lead in the passage from Matthew. In the elaboration of laws deriving from the Second Commandment, those relating to worldly affairs, Islamic jurisprudence also absorbed the principles of previous legal systems—Babylonian, Roman, and biblical—and other local laws, so much so that Muslim scholars regarded local pre-Islamic law (custom or local common law) as a secondary source of law when it did not contradict the Quran and the *Hadith*. This is how a lot of pre-Islamic practices—even such horrible ones as female genital cutting, a pre-Islamic African practice still performed in Egypt, Sudan, and Somalia—began in time to be regarded by Muslims as "Islamically required."

In a manner analogous to the development of American law over the past two centuries, Islamic law has grown over the past fourteen centuries. It includes the entire body of laws enacted by the many governments in Muslim lands and incorporates court rulings, first by the earliest caliphs and later by centuries of judges, many of which became established precedents, and the writings of legal scholars, which became Islamic jurisprudence, or *fiqh al-shariah*.

You will hear Muslims using the term *fiqh al-shariah* a lot. But Muslims also loosely use the term *Shariah* to refer to this enormous body of law throughout the centuries. This is like Americans calling the sum total of all American law in the past two centuries American constitutional law; it is correct in the sense that all American law has to abide by the Constitution, but it is incorrect to say that any given law is at the same level as the Constitution.

Take the example of speed limits on interstate highways. Suppose the federal government establishes a speed limit to reduce gas consumption and enhance passengers' safety. Such a law is constitutional. Do you violate the U.S. Constitution when you speed? No, you do not. You violate a law that derives its ultimate authority from the Constitution.

Since Shariah concerns itself with human life and safety, speed limits are also in accord with Shariah, by the way, even though there were no cars at the time of the Prophet. The analogous question for Muslims is, "Have you sinned against God when you exceed the speed limit?" The answer in this case is also no. You have broken a local law that derives its ultimate authority from God's law. But such questions are not always so easy to answer, even less so when people have practiced something for centuries and believe that the Quran requires them to do it. But in either case, it takes a method of legal reasoning to come to a conclusion.

Guided by and using principles of legal argument, Muslims arrive at decisions regarding all questions for which we cannot find explicit answers in the Quran and *Hadith*. That is why, for Muslims, law is so critical, and it is also why, when we face complicated social or religious questions, we go to the Quran, to the *Hadith*, and to our legal experts, scholars of Shariah.

As we deal with the new issues of twenty-first-century life, from modern medical dilemmas to issues like democracy and good governance, the role of women and matters of gender relations in contemporary times, and how to integrate ourselves as Muslims in American society, we can do so meaningfully *only* by mastering the tradition of Islamic legal thinking. Many self-appointed "leaders" who have not mastered this discourse are issuing fatwas anyway, causing great confusion and misleading millions. I am not saying that everyone must be a legal scholar. But Muslim religious leaders and thinkers have to ground their decisions in sound Islamic legal reasoning.

What Are the Objectives of Shariah?

Just as American constitutional scholars have always debated the intent of the framers (you may have heard the term "original intent" in many such discussions), Muslim legal scholars have also discussed the intent of God the Legislator. In analyzing Quranic commandments and those of the Prophet, whose decisions often helped flesh out many a Quranic commandment, understanding—or trying to understand—God's intent or objective in a given law is essential, because as we seek to apply the law in differing contexts, knowing God's intent helps us interpret and apply the law validly. This is all the more important as we engage important issues about how we Muslims can prosper as a faith community under the authority of American law and within American culture.

Muslim legal scholars unanimously agree that the overarching objective of Islamic law, its meta-objective, is to help realize the best interests of human beings in this life and the next. Scholars elaborated this fundamental purpose into six "objectives of the Shariah," or *maqasid al-shariah* in Arabic: six rights of all human beings that Shariah should protect and further: the rights to life, religion, mind (sound judgment, intellect, and well-being), property, family (marriage and progeny), and dignity.

More concretely, embedded in the right to life are the rights to food, shelter, clothing, health care, and personal security and safety. Religion implies the right of all religious communities to freely practice the religion of one's choice and prohibits religious discrimination. Rights associated with mind are the right to education, to pursue one's talents and psychological well-being, and protection from actions that erode mental capacity and judgment, such as intoxicants and drugs. Property rights are the right to be free of theft (that theft be deterred), to be able to own property, and to freely pursue wealth and economic security. The right to family includes the right to marriage, to sexual gratification, to children, and to family life and protection from adultery. Dignity implies the right to be free of oppression, to live in a well-governed society, and not to be enslaved, treated poorly, or discriminated against.

Because the Second Commandment mandates fair and just treatment between human beings, the central idea of Islamic jurisprudence provides that people's well-being is critical and that their basic human needs must be met. If people cannot eat, drink, sleep, be sheltered and clothed, marry those they love and have a family life, worship and act out their beliefs, learn and apply their intellectual capacity, and live freely and with dignity, they are not being treated justly. In such cases the objectives of Shariah are thwarted because people's lives are thwarted. As a result, Islamic law focuses society's attention not only on "doing the right thing" and "doing no harm and receiving no harm" (*la darar wa la dirar*), but also on its obligation to help its individual members to positively satisfy their basic human needs, which in the West are called human rights. Helping people satisfy those needs is a good deed, a positive good. Islamic law goes even further: it *requires* us to help other human beings eat, find shelter, worship, get educated, live in a dignified manner, and get married. And where the state can help provide these six objectives, it should.

There Is More Than One Way to Be Correct

Despite many Muslims' notion that somehow Islamic law sprang full-grown from the Quran and the mind of the Prophet, in fact Islamic law absorbed pre-Islamic classifications of law: criminal law, the law of personal status, the law of contracts, laws of governance, and laws of nations (what we understand as international law).

Like Jewish law and Christian canon law, Islamic law is the effort Muslims exerted to make laws on Earth that are faithful to divine decrees and intent. Shariah constitutes a very large and highly developed body of rulings and interpretations stretching back fourteen centuries that has given rise to a number of different schools of interpretation.

You know the joke about asking two rabbis one question and getting five answers? That is a way of understanding the variations of interpretation in Islamic law. There are five major schools of Islamic law and several lesser ones, all of which consider the others to be "correct." They agree on core issues of faith; they read the same Quran and have the same essential worldview. Their disagreements are relatively minor: Should we break our fast of Ramadan exactly at sunset, or about twenty minutes later, as the sky darkens? Since God says in the Quran that when the call to prayer is made on Friday, we should stop our business, how are we to treat a business deal made during a time when there should be no business deals? (In Saudi Arabia and some other countries, all shops close for a good hour or two during Friday prayers, and most offices and businesses in Saudi Arabia take the day off.) Each school provides a different answer to these kinds of questions.

Think about the laws of the states of Connecticut, California, and Illinois. They all share a core set of values; they are all bound by the U.S. Constitution. You would recognize most of the laws as you travel from state to state, but due to their different histories and geographies and populations, the state courts developed different precedents, which became local state laws. In the United States, state laws differ on issues as significant as the death penalty and gay marriage, as well as when and how stores can sell alcohol, which has to do with states' religious heritage and differing interpretations of what is permitted on the Sabbath.

In the judgments of the U.S. Supreme Court, written dissents are a critical part of the jurisprudential tradition. They offer a public critique of majority rulings and help to provide a check on a majority's inclusion of implicit or explicit political considerations. Depending on the skill and force with which they are argued, dissents may be studied in law schools as much as the majority opinions. They may even become the basis for future majority opinions overturning the decision in question. Today in Dar al-Ifta', the office of Egypt's chief mufti, legal researchers are collecting the opinions, decisions, and judgments of all previous jurists of all schools of legal interpretation into a database which his office uses in determining modern fatwas.

In societies without a clear separation of powers and a transparent system of jurisprudence, courts become the instruments of state power, politics, and policy. In Islamic history, key jurists—such as Imam Ahmad ibn Hanbal—played an important role in providing some degree of checks and balances to the power of the caliphs.

As I was growing up, I met scholars of Islamic law from all over the Muslim and Western world through my father. I heard many academic discussions of theology and law around the dinner table. I had the privilege of hearing academics discussing their *doubts* about an interpretation or *disagreeing* about points of Islamic law. I saw their common recognition of a core set of principles and their well-defined, vigorous differences of opinion *and* mutual respect for opinions they disagreed with, especially if those opinions developed as a result of political pressure.

Throughout these discussions the scholars consistently maintained the position that it was entirely possible that the differing opinions were correct. They felt—deep down in the fiber of their being—that differences of opinion among constitutional or legal scholars were a sign that there was more than one way to be right. The judgment of a court has to be one decision; but, as in the words popularly attributed to the Prophet, differences of opinion are a sign of God's mercy. In any event, that was the understanding I was brought up with.

Unfortunately, today there are many Muslims, ordinary people as well as political and religious leaders, who believe that the interpretation *they* grew up with is the only one. By regarding legitimate differences of opinion as un-Islamic, they violate the Prophet's *Hadith,* creating an unmerciful religion in the process. What could be more un-Islamic, irreligious, or even blasphemous than practicing a religion in a way that denies the mercy of God?

A friend of mine in Washington, D.C., told me a story when he learned I was the son of Dr. Muhammad Abdul Rauf, with whom he took *shahada* (made his first testimony of faith) when my father was director of the Islamic Center in D.C. He had asked my father a question, a question he no longer even remembers, but he will never forget my father's answer. My father told him that according to Imam al-Shafii's opinion it was such and such; according to Imam Malik's opinion it was something else; in Imam Abu Hanifa's it was still otherwise. But, my father added, he preferred Imam Malik's position in this particular case because of these reasons. (Jews may recognize a kind of Talmudic reasoning here.) The fact that he offered a menu of answers remains the most important lesson for my friend.

There are, for example, different schools of thought regarding how much of a woman's body should be covered during prayer or when in public. Understanding these differences is relevant to whether women's wearing the hijab (the headscarf) is a requirement or not. A firm and committed advocate of one of these schools should, in the course of making his argument, allow that the other point of view is also legally valid, as long as it proceeds from Islamic legal principles and employs Islamic jurisprudential method in arriving at its conclusion. If we follow one interpretation, we are required to recognize the validity of and to acknowledge and respect the differing interpretation of another school of law. This principle, alas, is observed far less frequently now than it was a century ago. Instead I often hear stories of men admonishing women that they will burn in hell if they do not wear a hijab!

This *hadith* should give pause to all who claim unerring certainty in their interpretations. The Prophet said:

> There were two aspirants from the Children of Israel, who were like brothers. One of them was in sin, the other strove in his worship. The pious fellow saw his colleague continuing sinning and advised

> him to desist. Still seeing him sinning one day, he again told him to desist. The sinner said "Leave me with my Lord. Were you sent to watch over me?" The other retorted: "By God! God will not forgive you nor admit you into Paradise!"
>
> So God took their souls, and they were brought [on Judgment Day] together before the Lord of Worlds, Who said to the aspiring pious fellow: "Do You know Me that well?" or "Are you the dispenser of what is in My Hands?" and told the sinner "Enter Paradise by My Mercy," and instructed the angels to drag the aspirant devotee to Hell. (Abu Dawud 4237)

Can Shariah Be Amended?

Just as the Constitution makes provisions for its own amendment, we know on the authority of the Quran itself that God has historically amended His own commandments from one prophet to another, from one era to another. And—this will come as a surprise to many Muslims—during the time of the Prophet, we know that the Quran abrogated or superseded some verses by means of later ones, demonstrating on the highest authority—God the Creator and ultimate Legislator Himself—that *context plays a central role in the determination of law and the application of commandments.* Indeed the Prophet is known to have made different decisions for different people based on context and circumstances.

Moreover, after the death of the Prophet Muhammad, we know that his second successor, Caliph Umar al-Khattab, the Prophet's father-in-law, who ruled during ten of the first dozen years after the Prophet's death and established very significant precedents in Muslim history, suspended the Quranic mandate of paying people to encourage their conversion to Islam. (Known as the *mu'allafati qulubuhum*—and mentioned in Quran 9:60—this practice was in many cases meant to compensate them for their losses in leaving behind their homes, property, and livelihoods in Mecca when they joined the Prophet in Medina.) Caliph Umar even suspended the penalty for theft in a time of famine because, he decided, the need to feed oneself in order to survive trumped the sin of theft.

Many contemporary Muslims, however, believe that every commandment, no matter how minor, no matter how culturally contextual, is eternally applicable to all contexts. This notion, however, is powerfully contradicted by historical judicial practice. Note that these contextual changes were all made in areas of Second Commandment law. Acts of worship were not considered changeable, for the relationship between God and man is eternal and unchanging.

Like the Quran, the U.S. Constitution stands above all later legislation and jurisprudence. In theory at least, the Supreme Court can reverse a century-old precedent, since it alone is the final legal arbiter of constitutionality. But the Court cannot argue that the Constitution itself is mistaken and must be revised. The framers, in their wisdom, made that bar quite high, requiring a two-thirds majority in both houses of Congress, as well as the approval of three-quarters of the states, in order to amend the Constitution.

Similarly Muslim jurists regard it as possible to revise or reverse precedent based on legal argument or to interpret the context of a Quranic or prophetic ruling to determine applicability to modern times, and even to indefinitely suspend a Quranic ruling, as Caliph Umar did. That we may do. But no Muslim can argue that the Quran or the *Hadith* was mistaken and therefore needs revision. Moreover the Quran, unlike the U.S. Constitution, is not primarily a legal document; it is divine revelation. So Muslims will never tamper with it or change any part of it. Also the Quranic text we read today is a historical document: abrogated legal verses remain part of the Quran along with the superseding verses. But as we saw previously, from the very earliest times Muslim jurists recognized the importance of context in interpreting, applying, or temporarily or even indefinitely suspending a Quranic commandment. This provides us with a powerful rationale to consider suspending punishments of the Shariah penal code, certainly in the West, where we have to abide by Western law, but also in Muslim majority societies.

In a seminal case, the chief justice of Baghdad Abu Yusuf, who died in 798 CE (166 years after the Prophet died), held that a ruling of the Prophet in a decision shaped by cultural context—in this case the fact that grain had been measured by volume in the time of the Prophet—could change as the cultural context changed, since in eighth-century Baghdad it had become customary to measure grain by weight and not by volume. Worldly law, in other words, did not have to remain tied to cultural practices of the Prophet's time.

This decision went far beyond the widely agreed upon principle that pre-Islamic custom or the common law of a given society is legally valid when it does not contradict Shariah (the Quran and *Hadith*); here the ruling is that *when a Shariah law is shaped by context, and the context changes, the law may change.* This contributed to why we have different interpretations in inheritance law, laws of governance, and contract law in different countries. This sophisticated understanding of Shariah is helpful to contemporary Islamic jurists as they grapple with modern questions in a globalized era. By the eleventh century, four centuries after the Prophet's death, Muslim jurists had developed a refined and highly nuanced jurisprudence that established justice as the overarching objective of Shariah and factored social context into their decision making.

So, are all earlier prescriptions of Shariah valid for today? Our predecessors delved into divine intent; they recognized justice as the supreme objective of Shariah and interpreted laws in that light. The challenge for our scholars today in America is to do what our predecessors did in their era, namely to produce a juristic understanding of Islamic law that is relevant to our American context.

We have been equipped with profoundly sophisticated Islamic legal reasoning devices to examine divine sources and deal with contemporary social questions in meaningful, substantive, and legally valid ways that genuinely appeal to the hearts of most Muslims and do not make them feel that we are sweeping their questions under the rug. I have used these principles to probe into and arrive at decisions that I believe are legally sound and helpful for our community of sincere believers.

Shariah and the Penal Code

Some Americans fear that Shariah is a set of seventh-century punishments Muslims want to bring to America. The truth is that apart from the penal code, Muslims practice Shariah law all the time in this country. All the time. Every time a Muslim prays, whether inside or outside a mosque; every time she donates to her community; every time he bears witness that there is no God but God and Muhammad is His Messenger; every time she fasts during Ramadan; every time he takes his child to school; every time he eats meat that has been slaughtered so as to be *halal*; every time she disposes of property in her will; every time an imam like me conducts a Muslim wedding according to the laws of any state in the union; every time we bury our dead in simple, environmentally friendly pine boxes and pray over them in accordance with our faith—we are observing and fulfilling Shariah law.

Unfortunately some have come to assume that the most brutal penal codes in the world are associated with Islam, when the truth is that most countries' penal codes in previous centuries were brutal by modern terms. The biblical punishment for adultery was stoning, but there are few op-ed articles in mainstream newspapers accusing Jews of legalized brutality. English common law provided for unimaginably cruel and painful public punishments—tearing flesh off criminals with red-hot metal tools, for example—for minor property crimes as recently as the eighteenth century, but no respectable legal scholar argues that we need a new foundation for American criminal law since it is based on that of our brutal English forebears. Singapore's practice of caning originated in that country's British colonial past, not its multireligious present. *Ling Chi,* the Chinese punishment known as "death by a thousand cuts" or "slow slicing," survived in that largely Confucian country until the early twentieth century.

There are very few Muslim societies that seek to apply the ancient penal code literally—in general only in those countries that have undergone a fundamentalist Islamic revival, such as the Taliban in Afghanistan or Wahhabism in Saudi Arabia. In the great majority of the Muslim world—in Indonesia, Malaysia, Turkey, and most of Africa—no adulterers are stoned to death, and not because there is no adultery.

Islamic law has important principles that guide it in providing justice. Punishment is not at all about the application of cruelty; it is rather about deterring or correcting the crime (or the results of the crime) that has already taken place. That is why, under Islamic law, compensating the family of a murder victim or the victim of theft or assault by returning stolen items or providing financial recompense is an important way of meting out justice.

Providing justice is a critical part of determining penalties for crimes. What Shariah seeks to accomplish through its penal code is to ensure the collective dignity and safety of a society. We do not punish criminals in order to take revenge on criminal behavior, but so that people can walk the streets and live in their homes safely, enjoying their freedoms and their rights.

The objective of both U.S. criminal law and Shariah penal law is to deter crimes and ensure society's safety, and to do so as mercifully as possible. God says in the Quran (2:179) that the punishments for these major crimes are intended to enhance life. As this is their stated divine intent, we are on solid ground in saying that if we can come up with new ways to achieve these objectives, we would be fully in compliance with Shariah's eternal intent: namely that justice be served, that people are safe, and that life and quality of life are enhanced. Because the term *hudud,* which refers to such punishments as stoning, is a word that also means "limits," many Muslim jurists have argued that the severe penalties, the *hudud* punishments in the Shariah penal code, are in fact meant as maximum punishments rather than mandatory ones. After all, most countries' criminal codes—including the Shariah criminal code—provide for maximum penalties (sometimes minimum ones as well) and give judges wide discretion as they impose penalties in individual cases. A society in which no punishments are meted out because people act justly and do not sin is a better society than one in which people are punished because they sin and act unjustly.

Another principle of Shariah is that no individual Muslim is allowed to take the law into his or her own hands and dispense punishment. Only courts can judge crimes and decree punishments; no one person can be the witness to a crime, its judge, and the implementer of the penalty—they must be separate individuals. Vigilante justice is therefore prohibited. This is one more reason, among many, why suicide bombing is utterly contrary to Islamic law, and why the murderers of Daniel Pearl and the assassins of thousands of innocent Iraqis, Afghans, and Pakistanis deserve the unanimous condemnation of Muslims everywhere.

I have been talking about Second Commandment violations, but what about violations of the First Commandment, crimes *only* against God? Precisely because they are sins only against God, God did not grant humans jurisdiction to penalize these sins. We human beings have no jurisdiction over them, and therefore the penal code in Shariah law has no provisions—none at all!—for punishing disbelief in God, not praying, not fasting during Ramadan, or never even considering going on the *hajj.* (Charity, although considered an act of worship, is a little different because it does affect society. And just as the U.S. government will pursue citizens for nonpayment of taxes, the first caliph, Abu Bakr, went to battle against a tribe that had refused to pay the *zakat.*)

Eating pork falls in the same category of sins only against God, since no other human is affected by it; thus there is no punishment for consuming pork. Only God has jurisdiction to punish sins against Him, which we believe will happen on Judgment Day. It would be difficult to overemphasize this principle. We do consider these acts sins, but they are sins against God, and human beings cannot presume the jurisdictional capacity to punish sins against God.

One example that confuses many is the putative penalty for apostasy, which in the *Hadith* was indeed in some cases capital punishment. But every one of these examples is drawn from when the Prophet and his community of believers were at war. Medina, led by the Prophet, was at war with Mecca. Apostasy then did not mean simply losing one's faith in God. Apostates in these cases went over to the other side and fought against the nascent Muslim community; they committed treason in time of war. Since most countries, including the United States, consider treason during wartime a capital offense, it is hardly surprising that early Muslims did as well.

Many Muslims today wrongfully assume, however, that any apostasy is a capital offense. In fact this conclusion represents a conflation of two different sins: treason, which remains a capital offense, and apostasy, which human beings do not have the jurisdiction to punish. According to my late friend Professor Mahmood Ghazi, a justice of the Supreme Shariah Court of Pakistan, "*apostasy simpliciter*," simple loss of belief outside of wartime, is not punishable by human beings—punishment lies in God's jurisdiction. And this is proven by the fact that when the Prophet negotiated the truce of Hudaybiyah, between the Muslims in Medina and the Meccans who were persecuting them, he agreed in writing to allow Muslims who had chosen to apostatize to freely return to Mecca unmolested.

Sins against other human beings lie in both jurisdictions, since they run counter to God's law *and* hurt other human beings. Therefore, in courts with due process, human beings are empowered to punish crimes and sins that lie within their jurisdiction to the extent that the sin hurts other people, their interests, or the larger community. Such punishable acts are murder, theft, slander, assault, property destruction, cruelty to animals, and environmental degradation.

Applying this rule is essential in fathoming the punishment for the consumption of alcohol. It is widely known that Muslims do not drink alcohol. And yet the prohibition on drink, which came relatively late in the Prophet's career, *carries no penalty in the Quran or the Hadith.* There were even companions of the Prophet who drank. Drinking was not an issue until a problem arose, in one particular case, after the Prophet's death, when one of these companions got drunk and walked the streets of Medina shouting slanderous things about some of the members of Medinan society. So Caliph Umar, who ruled at the time, convened a group of experts who eventually decided on a penalty. Since he had committed slander, they applied the penalty for slander.

Many scholars argue, as previously mentioned, that such penalties were in fact meant to be maximum, rather than mandatory, punishments, which allowed courts to take mitigating circumstances into account.

In 2009 a young woman in Malaysia was hauled before the Shariah court because she consumed a beer with some friends. It became a cause célèbre because the Shariah judge applied the maximum penalty of the law on the books, fining her RM5,000 (about U.S. $1,500) and six strokes of a cane. I wrote an op-ed piece for the local newspaper, *The Star,* arguing that the law on this matter should be revised to be consonant with the Quran, the *Hadith,* and this key bit of history. There was no evidence that the woman had committed any slander, and even if she had, I quoted the Quranic verse 24:22 (and its history) that urged the victim of slander to forgive the slanderer—all to make the point that being quick to punish is not the intent of the Shariah. Had there been cars during Caliph Umar's time, I suggested, and a drunken man ran his car over some pedestrians and killed them, he would have been charged with manslaughter. But would manslaughter also be charged against someone who had simply fallen on the street in a drunken stupor, having hurt no one but himself?

In America we apply such legal understandings all the time; there is no penalty for consumption of alcohol, but there is a fine for driving under the influence, and a greater penalty for killing someone while driving drunk. People do commit a variety of sins under the influence of alcohol, and proper application of any law, including Shariah, separates the act of drinking from the crimes committed under its influence, such as running someone over in a car. Even so, many Muslims today are absolutely convinced that the maximum penalty for slander is the Quranic punishment for drinking. It is bad enough that Muslims casually assume that a present punishment in a Muslim-majority country must have Quranic justification. Far worse is when our judges and jurists exhibit ignorance of the law or a misunderstanding that can—and usually does—result in the gross miscarriage of justice, and of Shariah, emphasizing a culture of punishment, of "do nots," instead of developing a culture of justice and mercy based upon educating people and doing the right thing. In Quran 18:103–4 God says that those who lose most are those whose efforts go astray in this world, while they think they are doing right. Only the extremists in any religion are keen to punish.

When extremist governments like the Taliban brutalize their citizens with self-righteous claims about Shariah, they are in fact violating the principles of Shariah. To use a word coined by a Christian minister friend of mine in New York, these are "punishmentalists."

It is a principle of Islamic jurisprudence that punishment cannot be meted out if the corresponding basic need is not met. I have already explained that Caliph Umar suspended the penalty for theft in a time of famine. This is why I have been incensed by recent incidents in Afghanistan. In July 2011 a young Afghan teenage couple fell in love and were nearly killed by their community. A year earlier, another young couple fell in love and eloped—and were stoned to death by their community, including family members. One of the *New York Times* articles on the incidents described the killing as "a brutal application of Shariah law," whereas in fact it was a *violation* of Shariah law. My guess is that if Caliph Umar were alive, he would have married them to each other and penalized the parents for trying to have the teenagers punished. (In the incident for which Caliph Umar suspended the penalty for theft, it was a claim by a man against his nephew, who stole his cloak during a time of famine. Not only did Umar not penalize the thief; he had the uncle punished for not having seen to his nephew's needs.)

The Islam that I grew up with, the Islam of the great majority of the world's Muslims and the Islamic jurisprudence of nearly a millennium and a half of study and debate, demands that Muslims adapt themselves to contemporary cultures and circumstances—and laws. I will go a step further. Given the Shariah principle that Muslims living in a country are required to adhere to the law of the land, Muslims today should never seek to enforce punishments in place over a thousand years ago when they violate the laws of the country in which they live. In that context, I believe it is time for Muslims to address the subject of the death penalty.

Shariah and the Death Penalty

The foundational text in considering this matter comes from the story of Cain and Abel, the first fratricide in the Bible and the Quran, after which God says, "For this reason We prescribed for the Children of Israel that whoever kills a person without his having killed or for his act of evil on earth, it is as if he has killed all of humankind; and whoever saves a life [literally 'gives life to a soul'], it is as if he has saved [or 'given life to'] all of humankind" (Quran 5:32). While the passage is usually cited as justification for killing a person—for having killed or for evildoing—the second half of the passage goes in quite a different direction.

Taking another's life is such a risky business that even at the price of sacrificing one's own life—as Abel did by not defending himself against Cain—it is better (from a Judgment Day point of view) to follow Abel's approach and not to kill. For if we kill one innocent person, it is if we have "killed all of humankind"—a terrifying prospect, and a responsibility no human being should ever have to shoulder. And yet our courts in America require judges, lawyers, juries, prison guards, and executioners to bear precisely that burden.

Moreover look what God promises to those of us who *save* a life: it is as though we have "saved all of humankind." Given the danger and the promise, shouldn't we all be working to save lives with all of our strength?

Should murderers be put to death? The Prophet gave us precedents for dealing quite differently with the sin of murder, using both forgiveness and monetary compensation. The Prophet himself forgave a man named Wahshi for having killed his uncle Hamza in the Battle of Uhud. After the conquest of Mecca, the Prophet not only forgave the city, but even after years of hostility, persecution of Muslims, and war he also forgave all those who had killed Muslims in war. Perhaps most striking of all for the time, when the Prophet Muhammad entered Mecca as its conqueror, his forces shed not a single drop of blood. They raped no women, pillaged no houses, destroyed no property. Instead the Prophet expressed gratitude to God that his service to God had achieved a positive victory on behalf of the faith. Of what modern conquering army can we make the same observation?

In his farewell sermon, the Prophet banned the Arab practice of blood revenge, protecting one's honor by killing the killer of a family member or relative, a pre-Islamic practice that is still practiced in some regions of the Muslim world (Muslim 2129).

Since 1977, when the death penalty was reinstated in the United States, the judicial system has spent hundreds of millions of dollars trying capital cases (in which most defendants do not receive the death penalty), housing death row inmates, and carrying out executions. States would be acting far more compassionately toward the victims of crime if they used some portion of these funds to compensate the families for their losses and injuries.

All over the world, including in the Muslim world, capital punishment is never applied uniformly in all segments or classes of society. Wealthy or politically connected individuals are often able to protect themselves, so capital punishment is mostly imposed on the weaker segments of society who cannot obtain adequate legal representation or who do not have the right connections to escape this most serious of punishments. In the United States, for example, in October 2011, 54 percent of death row inmates were black or Latino. While African Americans make up about 13 percent of the U.S. population, they account for 42 percent of inmates sentenced to death.

In the Muslim world, it is clear that serious punishments are frequently applied differentially by gender or by social class. In the rare cases of stoning for adultery it is nearly always the woman and not the man who is punished. Even though rape occurs in the Muslim world, rarely do we hear of a man accused of rape being stoned to death; we are more likely to hear of a rape victim being (falsely) accused of adultery. We also know that male homosexual rape (of young boys by those with authority over them) is more frequent than anyone wants to admit in some Muslim-majority countries, such as Afghanistan and Pakistan. But hardly ever do we hear of instances of homosexual rapists being caught and punished.

During the Prophet's time in seventh-century Arabia there were no law enforcement agencies and no system of jails and prisons to punish murderers and other criminals by removing them from society. Today we have such systems and infrastructure, and it is worth revisiting punishments at the time of the Prophet in the light of these changed circumstances. Many Muslim-majority countries have done just that, and a growing number either do not provide for capital punishment (such as Bosnia, Turkey, and Senegal), or do not apply it even though the punishment remains on the books (Algeria, Morocco, Tunisia, Mali, Niger).

Replacing capital punishment with life imprisonment without parole helps ensure that no government commits the crime of killing an innocent person. In the United States alone, between 1973 and

October 2010, there were 173 exonerations of Death Row inmates. That is to say, a state was preparing to execute someone innocent of the crime. Of the 1,272 executions since 1977, how many of those were carried out on innocent persons? If killing an innocent person is truly, as God said, the equivalent of killing all of humankind, how can we take such a risk? How can we ask anyone to take responsibility for such a potential catastrophe?

"Saving a life is like saving all of humankind," God says (Quran 5:32). By banning capital punishment, we will save many innocent human lives, each of which is equivalent to *saving all of humankind.* And by replacing capital punishment with life imprisonment for the genuinely guilty soul, we may help save his soul as well by giving him the chance to repent. Many a saint was a sinner: Christianity's St. Augustine, Islam's Umar al-Khattab (who wanted to kill the Prophet), Khalid bin al-Walid (who fought the Prophet before accepting Islam, and then killed a Muslim). All were transformed and became among the greatest exponents and teachers of their faith. Since giving sinners the chance to repent is an Islamic imperative, giving criminals the opportunity to repent is an ever greater act of good, an even stronger Islamic imperative.

In the United States many non-Muslims convert to Islam in prison, the most famous being Malcolm X. In a prison I visited with my father in the late 1960s, I remember meeting an inmate who was not only serving a life sentence, he had converted to Islam and was serving as the imam of that prison's Muslim community.

Thinking with Shariah

There are a few basic principles of Islamic legal reasoning that will go a long way toward helping American Muslims adapt to the American context and helping Muslims—and non-Muslims—to think calmly and rationally about Shariah.

First, and perhaps most important of all, is that God's *intent* for a law always trumps the *letter* of the law. God doesn't always tell us the reason for a law (such as the prohibition on eating pork). Therefore, although we can speculate on the reason (the danger of contracting trichinosis), when no intent is given the general ruling is that we follow the letter of the law. But when God *does* give us the reason for the law, then it is wrong to adhere to the letter of the law if in so doing we violate the intent. That would be like insisting that an ambulance carrying a heart attack victim to the hospital abide by traffic regulations such as speed limits and stopping at red lights "because it's the law." It is the law, but the *purpose* of speed limits is to save lives, and in those cases when you need to save a life by breaking the speed limit, the right decision is to get the patient to the hospital as quickly as possible. Again, the purpose of the law always trumps the letter of the law.

A second principle is that whatever is not explicitly prohibited in the Quran or the *Hadith* is de facto permitted. As obvious as this might be logically, you will be surprised how many Muslims come to me asking if such and such an act is permitted. They are looking for a list of permitted actions. I tell them that the list is infinite. All we have to do is look at the list of prohibited acts, and if the act in question is not on that list, it is permitted. Thus far more is permitted or encouraged than is prohibited. There are different categories of permission and prohibition that will easily make sense to you. There are obligations (such as performing prayers, being just and working for justice, treating people with mercy); preferred or encouraged actions (additional prayers, additional charity); neutrally permitted actions (drinking tea or coffee at breakfast); discouraged or disliked actions (smoking); and those that are prohibited—*haraam* in Arabic. The category *haraam* includes both relatively minor prohibitions (drinking alcohol, eating pork) and the major sins of murder, theft, and adultery. Interestingly there are times when and places where the Prophet forbade prayers and days when fasting is forbidden. Such prohibitions underline the notion of not being excessive in our religiosity, as well as the importance of context in determining the rightness of an action.

Where the Quran and the *Hadith* are silent we are encouraged to extrapolate by analogy from Quranic rulings and principles and Quranic verses and *Hadith* that might be applicable. Jurists generally agree that after the Quran and *Hadith,* the consensus of legal scholars and arguments by analogy comprise the major sources of laws. Secondary sources include the customary law of a given society, legislation by the legislative branch of a government, and judicial decisions that become legal precedents. Muslim jurists were quite clear on the principle that the institutions, laws, and customs of the people were by definition normative as long as they did not contradict the Quran and *Hadith.* Such principles can take you a long way in questions of finance, sexuality, health, psychology, diet, interpersonal relationships, popular culture, clothing, fashion, and politics.

A third principle in Islamic jurisprudence is that necessity can make the forbidden permitted, but only for the amount and duration of the necessity (Quran 2:173). Let me give an example. Suppose that my child, or I, have a bad cough that is keeping everyone in my family awake at night, making for a whole group of irritable children and parents. Most cough syrup contains alcohol, which tends to put children out for the night. Are we allowed to partake of an alcohol-based cough medicine? In the case of taking medicine to heal ourselves, we are not only allowed, but *required* to do something that in another context would be considered *haraam,* or forbidden.

How strong is the necessity, one might ask, and how long would the necessity continue? If your only choice, in confinement, say, is between eating pork or starving to death, legal scholars would expect you to eat. But if it were simply a matter of missing a meal or two, the legal opinion would come out on the other side.

A fourth basic principle is the importance of context, which of course is critical to Western legal systems as well. The act of taking a human life, for example, has one status in war, when it is not a crime, and another when it is gratuitous or for monetary gain, say, in which case it may be murder. And it has yet a different status if it is accidental: for example, if you were to lose control of your car on an ice slick, skid, and inadvertently kill a pedestrian. All legal systems permit taking a life in self-defense as well. Context can determine right or wrong, but people lose sight of this obvious fact all the time. Take dress, for instance, or its absence. No religious or secular law in the world prohibits consenting spouses from being nude in each other's private company. Nearly all legal systems, however, prohibit nudity on public streets and in schools.

A fifth principle is that not all sins are equal, and neither are all good deeds equal. We need to behave in such a way that we don't commit the big sins and are merciful with one another regarding the small ones. There are Quranic verses (4:31, 53:31–32) to the effect that God will overlook our smaller errors if we are careful not to commit large sins. It is not that God wants us to behave badly. Rather the much larger problem is that people spend an inordinate amount of time worrying about the small sins, while freely engaging in big ones. Unfortunately, many Muslims hold to the misunderstanding that all sins and all positive commandments are equally important. Recall that Jesus, who in his own words came to fulfill the law, reminded us that there are in fact two *greatest* commandments on which "hang all the law and the prophets," meaning thereby that the other commandments are lesser ones.

If we Americans—Christians, Jews, and Muslims—accept God's assertion in our respective scriptures that humanity was created from one man and one woman, then we are all of one family and equal in the eyes of God, distinguished only by our piety and our ethics. A clear ethical vision, a commitment to human faithfulness and justice that is neither wishy-washy nor unafraid of bold pronouncement, shines brightly through our religious laws, our American constitutional law, and Shariah. This spiritual and ethical vision ought to manifest itself in every way we engage with others: in our business and political relationships, in our dealings with friends and family, and in our relationship to God.

Islam and Shariah in Different Cultures

Muslims in America hail from Bangladesh to Senegal, Morocco to Iran, and Egypt to Indonesia. You may ask, therefore, Is there such a thing as a Bangladeshi or Senegalese or Iranian or Indonesian—and therefore an American—Islam and Shariah? In terms of core theology and liturgical practice, the answer is no. We all believe in one Quran, one God, the *Hadith,* and the principles of law; we pray the same way, in the same language; we fast in the same month, give charity, and perform the *hajj* in the same manner in the same places in and around Mecca.

But it is equally true that as Islam spread from the Arabian Peninsula to Egypt and across North Africa to sub-Saharan Africa and to what are now Turkey, Iran, India, Bangladesh, Pakistan, and Indonesia, it expressed itself in the institutional, cultural, and legal forms and norms of those societies. And in those countries we see culturally specific differences in clothing, in music, in architecture, even in law and customs.

Growing up in Malaysia and going back to Egypt for holidays, I could see both the commonalities and the differences of Muslim life in those two countries. Islam has penetrated the Malaysian mind-set so much that the Malays are the only people I know of in the world who literally equate ethnic "Malayness" with Islam; an ethnic Malay is constitutionally a Muslim. When someone converted to Islam, Malays used to say he entered "Malayness": *masok Melayu.* Malaysia provides an excellent example of how pre-Islamic law, common law, and custom were recognized by Shariah Law; to Malays, the expression *adat Melayu* (Malay custom), a term that came out of Shariah terminology, survived and continues as Malay law.

Once a Somali scholar visited us in our home in Malaysia. After dinner my father requested that he recite a few verses from the Quran and some religious songs. I could hear the cadences of sub-Saharan Africa in his voice as he recited and sang, so different from Egyptian chanting and music. But it was not until I came to New York that I began to experience the broadest range of Muslim culture. I will never forget the first year we arrived; in his mosque, my father asked an elderly African American gentleman, Ahmad Hashim, to call the *adhan,* and I heard American jazz and blues in his call. When I was in graduate school, my Pakistani friend Shahid Akhtar introduced me to *qawwali,* a type of Sufi singing from India and Pakistan that put me on the verge of a trance. A friend gave me a record of a South African Sufi group whose music actually did put me into a trance state. And today my friend Adamu (James "Blood" Ulmer), a well-known jazz electric guitarist, captivates me, as he does his fans all over the world, by playing the music he hears in the recitation of the Quran in Arabic. In all these instances I see the universal Islamic impulse expressed in the local cultural genius.

Sometimes a local culture pushes back, as in 2009, when the citizens of Switzerland passed an amendment to the federal constitution banning the construction of minarets, the spires frequently built on mosques and from which the call to prayer issues, nowadays generally through loudspeakers. It so happens, however, that at the time, of the roughly 150 mosques and prayer spaces in Switzerland, only four had minarets, according to the *New York Times,* and "none conduct the call to prayer." The reason given by the political party that sponsored the proposal was that minarets were a symbol of Islamic law—which it sought to demonize. The public campaign against minarets was clearly meant as a rebuke (at best) to Muslims, as the campaign was nasty and fearmongering. Muslims and their supporters argued against the ban on the grounds of religious freedom and because the campaign was clearly Islamophobic.

But it is worth pointing out that there is nothing Quranic about a minaret. The Quran is silent on the subject, and the Prophet himself said nothing at all. In fact the Prophet's original mosque in Medina had no dome and no minaret. It had a thatched roof of palm fronds and mud bricks. It was only after a couple of centuries that Muslims began constructing mosques with domes and minarets, which the muezzin would climb to chant the call.

Contrary to what many think, Muslim architects did not invent the domes; as mentioned in the introduction, they adapted them from Byzantine churches, such as the Greek Orthodox Hagia Sophia in what was then Constantinople and is now Istanbul. One of the most famous mosques in the Holy Land, the Dome of the Rock, was modeled on the Church of the Holy Sepulcher in the Old City of Jerusalem (where Jesus was said to be crucified) and to this day has no minaret.

Muslims eventually rebuilt the Prophet's mosque, adding a dome and a minaret. Now even most Muslims think a mosque *must* have a dome and a minaret, when there is nothing in Islamic law requiring either one, and the history makes clear that the dome itself was an adaptation of Christian architecture. (Some believe that domed churches were themselves modeled on the Second Jewish Temple in Jerusalem, the site of the Dome of the Rock.)

There is simply no reason a mosque in Switzerland should have to look like a mosque in Egypt. I argued at the time, not entirely jokingly, that a Swiss mosque should resemble a genuine Swiss icon—a Swiss cheese, for instance, with windows for the holes, or a cuckoo clock calling the prayer time five times a day. Chinese mosques, after all, resemble other temples in China, with curved roofs and pagoda-like structures. Take a look at them online; they are quite beautiful, and unless you are Chinese, you would never guess they were mosques. Why should Swiss mosques be any different? By establishing community committees that include representatives of the other faith traditions and political leaders from both the Muslim and non-Muslim communities to vet proposed designs for a Swiss mosque, Swiss Muslims could come up with designs that the whole community would not only endorse, but take pride in.

In America we can design mosques any way we please. My own mosque in Tribeca is a converted storefront, with no dome or minaret, and is no less a mosque for that. Certainly the mosque I envisioned in Cordoba House was not going to have either a dome or a minaret. My idea was to launch a contest among architects to design a uniquely American mosque. Some of our greatest architects have designed churches and synagogues; take a look online at Le Corbusier's Notre Dame du Haut. Why not mosques?

A mosque is not defined by what it looks like, but by the activities that take place in it and what it does for the community. Besides, most Muslims would happily trade their fancy architectural masterpieces to be able to go back in time and join the Prophet in his mud-floor and thatched-roof mosque.

Symbols are important to people, and we need to be sensitive to how people understand and respond to them. But by understanding how symbols were created in the past, religious leaders can educate both American Muslims and our non-Muslim neighbors, and together work to create new symbols that feel right for all. All religions that spread across more than one culture learn to express and re-create their spiritual, religious, legal, and artistic values and impulses in the local vernacular and vocabulary of local customs, traditions, dress, food, rituals, even beliefs. In human religious experience, adapting the local culture of a given country has been commonplace, and when that happens, people eventually regard that religion as native rather than alien.

As Christianity spread from Palestine through the Middle East and Europe, for example, it adapted to its new geographical and cultural homes very explicitly. Christians developed, among many other denominations, the Greek, Russian, and Syrian Orthodox Churches, the Coptic Christian Church in Egypt, the Roman Catholic Church in Rome and now Italy, and later the Dutch Reformed Church in Holland, the Anglican Church in England, and even the Reformed Church in America. Roman Catholics think of Christianity as more Italian than Palestinian. I sat on a panel a few weeks after 9/11 and heard an Arab Christian priest from Jordan say, "I am a Christian, but my culture is Muslim." The two major geographical-cultural groupings of Jews—Sephardic and Ashkenazi—draw their names, respectively, from Spain and Germany.

Of course none of this happened overnight, but similar experiences structured the spread of Islam, which took root and expressed itself in local cultural and institutional forms. Soon there appeared a Turkish, Indian, West African, Iranian, Indonesian, and Egyptian Islam. I use these names generally, because Muslims have retained the universal practice of their core beliefs and acts of worship throughout the Muslim world, but in terms of variations of laws, culture, art, architecture, and music, you can certainly see the distinctive national variants of Muslim practice.

When you see the vigorous Muslim promotion of cultural practices that seem extremely alien to a host culture, like the burka in France, say, you are seeing the influence of other factors: a desire to be recognized as Muslim, or Muslims asserting their civil rights or making a political statement, and not mainstream religious practice.

The Prophet himself prayed the noon and afternoon prayers in Mecca softly, not aloud, so as not to annoy the Meccan unbelievers; this practice continued, and still prevails today all over the world. Universally, noon and afternoon prayers are not recited aloud. (The Friday congregational prayer conducted at noon is the exception.) If he was so attuned to the feelings of his neighbors, shouldn't we Muslims, who assert that we seek to follow his *sunna,* also be considerate of the feelings of our neighbors and seek a classical interpretation of Shariah that is sensitive to them?

Bangladeshi Muslims, for example, have continued many pre-Islamic Hindu cultural practices, such as women wearing red saris at their weddings, putting a dot on their foreheads, touching the feet of their parents and elders (a Hindu tradition for acquiring the blessings of elders), none of which are practiced in the other parts of the Muslim world.

Or take the Iranian Muslim observation of the holiday of *Nowruz,* the first day of spring and the Iranian New Year. It may have been originally a Zoroastrian custom, but whatever its origins, it is undeniably a pre-Islamic holiday, which has nothing to do with Islam. Still, all Iranian Muslims celebrate it with great fanfare, just as Americans celebrate Thanksgiving. Turkish and Senegalese and Indonesian Muslims do not. A cultural event that brings people together—what could be wrong with that?

And yet just because Muslims practice or observe a holiday does not mean that it is Islamic—except in this extremely important sense: the Prophet's own adoption of Arab cultural practices makes it absolutely clear that it is a positive *good* to practice the cultural norms of a society as long as they do not contradict the Quran and the *Hadith*. To that end, we need to express Muslim theology and jurisprudence within American jurisprudence and law, American culture, American politics, American architecture, and even American musical forms. In that sense we can speak of an authentic American expression of Islam. And when that happens, Americans will begin to regard Islam as an *American* religion.

As Christians know, a profound part of Jesus' prophetic ministry was to criticize mistaking the *letter* of the law for the *intent* of the law. We mentioned earlier that Jesus said—objecting eloquently to the complex of rules determining what could not be done on the Sabbath—"The Sabbath was made for humankind, and not humankind for the Sabbath." Too many Muslims today are committing the same sins that our predecessors committed by equating the letter of the law to God. Law—or Shariah—is made for us, and not us for Shariah.

I do not minimize the occasional difficulty in deciding where to draw the line between what is cultural and what is religiously Islamic. Since many Muslims grow up in a particular culture, they tend to mix what is cultural and what is Quranic. When Muslims immigrate to the United States, they tend to bring their own cultural expressions wholesale. When that happens, Islam appears alien and foreign to Americans.

A similar thing happened when affluent Iranian Jews came to Great Neck, Long Island, in large numbers in the 1980s and 1990s, after the 1979 Iranian Revolution. An otherwise open-minded and generous Jewish acquaintance complained bitterly to me at the time about how the nouveau riche Iranian immigrants cut down old trees and renovated houses to look like those they had left in Iran, all the while casually triple-parking fancy cars in the village downtown, clogging the streets and raising the blood pressure of longer-term residents, many of whom were also Jewish. Culture, not surprisingly, turned out to be much stronger than religion.

There are things we Muslims can easily do if we want to be accepted quickly in America. Rather than making requests solely on our own behalf (for prayer space in a college, for instance), we could figure out how to make them on behalf of a larger group (all the faith groups on campus). For the more we contribute to the well-being of other Americans—and are perceived as doing so—the more successful we will be. And we can certainly announce our Americanness by accommodating Muslim dress codes of modesty to American fashion, rather than insisting on dressing as Egyptians, Indonesians, or Senegalese.

It is pressing, therefore, that we help our people understand what is eternal in Islam and what is contextual. God Himself states in the Quran that He sent His messages to different communities through messengers who spoke to the community in their own language; this certainly means culture and law too! It is not a matter of trimming our religious sails or smoothing over rough edges that may make our beliefs difficult for others. It is a serious process of figuring out who we are in America, this most modern and fast changing of countries, with the most vibrant, powerful—and at times coarse and threatening—popular culture in the world. As we do so, we need always to remember that whenever there is an apparent conflict between American law and Shariah, on the authority of Shariah itself American law holds.

3

ISLAM AND OTHER RELIGIONS

Muslims and Jews in New York

My first visit to a Jewish temple was with my father in New York City in 1967, when I was eighteen, just after the Six-Day War. I did not want to go. After all, I was the epitome of what Jews considered the enemy at the time: an Egyptian Arab Muslim. I was deeply uncomfortable. My father insisted, however, and I went.

Imam of the Islamic Centers of New York and of Washington, D.C., in the 1960s and 1970s, my father was a Muslim pioneer of what was known as the "ecumenical movement" of the era. He was one of the few Muslim leaders Jews could talk to across the often bitter feelings provoked by the Arab-Israeli conflict, and he spoke frequently in the pulpits of churches and synagogues. By his example he taught me that it is precisely during moments of crisis that people need to reach out the most. That is when interfaith dialogue and coalition building are most needed: in moments of emotional intensity, whether they be peaks or valleys.

Still, embarrassed by the military defeat and angry at the Jewish celebration of Israel's victory and the pain of many Egyptians killed, some of them relatives of ours, I was afraid that Jews just wanted to gloat. I was already getting into *very* heated arguments about Israel with my Jewish classmates at Columbia University. My father assumed something else: that at some level Jews wanted real dialogue with the other side in spite of their military victory. Later in life I saw that he was right.

But just because something is necessary does not make it easy to pull off. That war polarized Jewish-Muslim relations, when what we really needed was to reach out to each other. Another time I went with my dad to a synagogue, and he put on a yarmulke. I remember being really uncomfortable, upset, even angry. Engaging in dialogue was one thing, but putting on a Jewish religious garment? I had to ask him what on earth he was doing. I would like to think that there was no challenging or offensive tone in my voice, but in retrospect I am not so sure. I was trying to sort out my own identity, and these experiences were complicating matters. He said, very simply, that he did it out of respect for the congregation and their religion, and for the rabbi, his friend.

What a lesson that was for me: that political disagreements between our faith communities should not trump the faith relationship, which must run deeper. This was the lesson my father learned from the exemplary behavior of Caliph Umar. In spite of nasty political conflict between the nascent Muslim community and Jewish tribes in Medina during the war with Mecca some fifteen years earlier, soon after the Muslim conquest of Jerusalem in 637 he invited Jews to take up residence in the holy city; this was the first time they had been allowed in Jerusalem since being banished by Romans for 500 years; his invitation enabled them to fulfill their age-old aspiration "Next year in Jerusalem!" A corollary example was that of the great scholar and rabbi Moses Maimonides, who left his hometown of Cordoba because of persecution from the extremist Almohade dynasty. He took refuge in Morocco and later in Egypt, where he was welcomed, demonstrating that he did not regard political conflict with *some* Muslims as meaning he should regard *all* Muslims as enemies.

For Muslims Caliph Umar is a great exemplar, as Maimonides is for Jews. Neither of them would let politics polarize his relationships. We need to follow their examples, not the example of those who seek divisiveness across the globe.

Even before the Six-Day War my father had become friends with the legendary rabbi and scholar Louis Finkelstein, a longtime chancellor of the Jewish Theological Seminary on the Upper West Side of New York. Accompanying my father to visit Rabbi Finkelstein, I began to learn something about Jews and the Jewish community. Scholars had a sense of the theological and social history between the faith communities and scholarly traditions that a teenager like me still had to learn. Like many other young men and women, I was a victim of the emotional stirrings that politics can evoke in us. I realized that I believed a lot of myths about Jews, simply because I had not known any personally before coming to America. I thought of them as very foreign, very different, and I had assumed as a matter of course that they all hated Arabs and Muslims.

Plus, I came of age in the 1960s, at a time when the State of Israel was still very young. The dynamics between Israel and the Arab world shaped perceptions on both sides, in the same way that the perceptions of Russians and Americans brought up during the Cold War were entirely shaped by that conflict. Throughout the Arab world we thought of the founding of Israel as the *Nakba,* the great catastrophe. We thought of it primarily as a loss to Arab and Muslim dignity.

It was not until later that I saw how much of a loss this conflict created for Muslim and Jewish worlds alike, resulting in tremendous animosity between Muslims and Jews in Egypt and in many countries in the Middle East, where previously there had been good relationships. Because of centuries of living alongside local Jews in the Arab and Muslim world, Muslims and Arabs of my father's generation always differentiated between Jews and Zionists. They thought of Jews as those with whom they lived, as people of faith; Zionists were different, and were seen as a European Jewish political movement that intruded into the Middle East and spawned Jewish-Muslim hostility there and globally.

You may be surprised to learn that at no time growing up was I ever encouraged by my father or mother to use anti-Semitic slurs or to think in anti-Semitic stereotypes. These were simply not their ethics. Plus, Jews were part of our lives. My parents invited my younger sister's school principal, Mr. Cohen, to our home, and we became very good friends. Early on in our time in New York, an elderly Jewish couple, the Levitts, became very close to my parents. I learned that Jewish and Arab mothers share a love of cooking and feeding their families. The Levitts would regularly invite us to their home for meals and we would return the favor, and when I was in graduate school and my parents were in Washington, the Levitts would invite me several times a month for a meal. It was very natural; we enjoyed each other's company as friends.

My youngest brother was just four when we came to this country, and when he went to elementary school my mother befriended the mother of another boy at the school, a Greek Jewish woman who became one of her dearest friends. I remember the two of them cooking and introducing each other to Greek and Egyptian versions of moussaka. Friends and neighborly relations like these change your perception of people.

I also saw that, in the collective consciousness of the Jewish community, there was a great common desire to be accepted—and for Israel to be accepted—by the Arabs. American Jews wanted peace between Israel and its Arab neighbors, but no Arab political leader then appeared interested. The vast majority of the discourse in the Arab world, much of it articulated by Egypt's enormously influential nationalist leader Gamal Abdel Nasser, was all about denying Israel's right to exist.

That overwhelmingly hostile context provided the emotional and logical rationale for why my father was invited by members of the Jewish community to engage in dialogue. But for him, I think, he was simply following the Quran (49:13): "We have created you from one male and one female and made you peoples and tribes that you may know one another."

Several years after my father passed away in December 2004, I received a call from his dear friend Peter Stewart, the founder of Thanksgiving Square, the multifaith group based in Dallas that sponsors the National Prayer Breakfast. Peter invited me to speak at the Breakfast in Dallas. As much as I wanted to accept, I had to be overseas at that time, so out of his desire to recognize the role my father played in founding Thanksgiving Square with him, he extended the invitation to any member of the Rauf family. My wife, Daisy, who had become an avid multifaith advocate, went on the family's behalf; she would be the first woman ever to speak at the National Prayer Breakfast. She was given a tour of the museum before her lecture, and to her surprise saw photographs of my father, along with the ecumenical declaration (signed by him) establishing the vision for Thanksgiving Square. She was very moved and proud to be the daughter-in-law of a great luminary on whose shoulders we were both riding.

There may have been another reason that Jews reached out to my father. In America in the 1960s Islam was perceived through the lens of the Black Muslim movement. The African American version of Islam in this country at the time was led by Elijah Muhammad and Malcolm X , who offered an unabashed verbal assault on white racists and white racism—even going so far as to claim that the white race was the creation of a diabolical scientist named Yakub, the biblical Jacob.

Based mainly in big cities with large African American populations such as New York, Chicago, and Detroit, Black Muslims rejected the racial integration and voting rights strategy of the civil rights movement and preached African American control of local institutions. Unfortunately the black-Jewish alliance that had helped sustain the civil rights movement for a dozen years was falling apart, perhaps most spectacularly in New York during a 1968 citywide teachers' strike prompted by class, racial, and religious tensions centered in the African American neighborhoods of Ocean Hill and Brownsville. Jews went on the defensive with respect to African Americans as well as American Muslims.

Following my father's example, I began to befriend Jewish classmates in the late 1960s. In the fall of 1966 the Jewish Theological Seminary invited me to join an interfaith group they started. It was exciting and challenging. We wanted to establish a discourse on eternal principles of our faiths that could provide a framework for more discussion and discourse on a whole range of issues. That kind of conversation was almost nonexistent at the time. It helped that there were two lovely ladies there responsible for the programs, who were like aunts to me. They took us to Mohonk Mountain House, the beautiful hotel on Lake Mohonk in upstate New York, for weekend-long interfaith discussions.

The first time I went to Lake Mohonk for one of these interconversations was in October 1966, and I felt like I was in heaven. The fall coloring of the leaves was at its height. I had never seen such natural beauty. Ever since then Lake Mohonk has held a very special place in my heart. So have those discussions, which I have made a central part of my teachings in my mosque and my multifaith outreach work ever since.

God's Religion through Many Prophets: "Be Not Divided Therein"

The second page of the Quran (2:4) begins with God's insisting on the importance not only of the Quran itself, but also of all previous revelations to the "god-fearing," those "who believe in what has been sent down to thee [the Quran], and what has been sent down before thee [the Torah, Psalms, and Gospels]." Muslims believe that God's revelations to humankind began long before those to the Prophet Muhammad. We believe Adam was the very first prophet. As the youngest of the three Abrahamic faiths (the religions tracing their monotheistic origins to Abraham) and all global religions, Islam has always been understood by Muslims to be intimately connected to all its predecessors.

The importance of these words cannot be overstated. They have defined my understanding of Islam and the Quran and have been the foundation of my life's work, which I have dedicated to spreading the message they contain. Here God is saying that the Quran is part of a sacred line of divine revelations to human beings; previous revelations are not diminished in significance by the arrival of new revelations. The Quran, the newest revelation of God's words, explicitly affirms *what was said before.* Throughout the Quran, God insists on the multiplicity of prophets and messengers He has already sent throughout the world, speaking different languages but teaching one message. That is what my father was doing by going to synagogues and churches. He was not simply believing in the words of the Quran; he was putting them into practice. And his example has been an inspiration for my life's work.

The larger point I want to get across here is one that I suspect few Jews and Christians know about Muslims and their faith; many Muslims know it intellectually, but instead of internalizing it emotionally, spiritually, and practically, they have allowed political pressures to push it aside. In the Quran God says clearly that the revelations of the Torah and the Gospels and those to Muhammad are of a piece—not to be thought of as designed for different peoples: "He has ordained for you as your law [or as your religion] what He charged Noah with, and that which We have revealed to thee, and what We charged Abraham with, Moses and Jesus: Perform the religion, and scatter not regarding it" (Quran 42:13). God also says that He gave to each community "rites which they perform" (Quran 22:67) through messengers, each of whom was sent by God to speak to his people in his own language: "And We sent no Messenger but with the language of his people so that he might explain to them clearly" (Quran 14:4). Clearly then, whatever the differences between religions, they are more than offset by greater points of similarity that God Himself asserts.

Such beautiful ideas: first, "and scatter not regarding it," more often translated, almost as poetically, as "be not divided therein." To me the beauty of this passage lies in its insistence that at our core, we hold the same beliefs whether we follow Moses, Jesus, or Muhammad, or any of the hundreds of other prophets. Second, there are natural differences of time, language, and context that God Himself acknowledges. It is therefore no accident that some Christians refer to Satan as "the divider."

We are not, God says, to be divided in our performance of religion. We are not to regard each other as infidels, unbelievers, heretics, apostates, or idolaters. We are not to say to another faith adherent, "You are beyond the boundary of humanity," so that we can attack or kill him. Instead the variety in human belief is something we need to protect and embrace. Diversity itself is a matter of divine intent; we are not to scatter and become homogeneous insular communities. On the contrary, we are to make a genuine human community out of our diversity.

Just as a garden has many different flowers, not simply one variety or color, the most important work confronting all humanity, whatever our faiths, is to find the platform on which we can unite in spite of our differences—understanding that those differences are insignificant compared to our similarities, and that whatever our differences, we have an obligation to protect every other community. That is what characterizes America at its best—and we Muslims have our own responsibility to help create *unum* out of this *pluribus*.

The Abrahamic faiths are connected liturgically as well as scripturally. One only needs to remember that the Last Supper of Jesus was in fact a Passover Seder. For Muslims, according to our narratives, when the Prophet first went to Medina (before the commandment was revealed to fast during the month of Ramadan) he saw Jewish tribes fasting on the tenth day of the New Year, Yom Kippur. He asked why, and Muslim narratives report that he was told Moses fasted on that day to commemorate the day God saved the Children of Israel from the yoke of Pharaoh. In the Jewish tradition Yom Kippur, the Day of Atonement, commemorates Moses receiving the tablets on Mount Sinai.

Regardless, the more relevant point is that the Prophet, who regarded Moses as his brother, responded to the Medina Jews, "I am closer to Moses than you are," and fasted on that day as well in solidarity with Moses (Bukhari 1865). To this day Muslims observe this *sunna,* or practice, of the Prophet, and fast on Ashura, the tenth day of our New Year. (It also happens to be the anniversary of the assassination of the Prophet's grandson Hussein, which Shias observe on that day as well.)

You see, Muslims and Jews (and Christians) are authentic spiritual brothers and sisters, literally issued from the same father. How many Muslims fast the day of Ashura to follow the Prophet's *sunna* and forget that part of his inner *sunna,* his reason for fasting, was to express his solidarity with Moses—in our case perhaps as an expression of solidarity with devout Jews? A few years ago the first day of Ramadan coincided with Rosh Hashanah, the Jewish New Year. Ten days later, of course, Ashura coincided with Yom Kippur, the Jewish Day of Atonement (during which observant Jews fast). Our New York Muslim community experienced a wonderful kinship with a Jewish congregation, B'Nai Jeshurun, with whom we had been having interfaith dialogues, by breaking our fasts together at sundown on Yom Kippur during Ramadan. I think it would be wonderful if American Muslims continued to fast on Yom Kippur, even when it does not coincide with Ashura, to keep the Prophet's sentiment alive for our times. Perhaps some of my Jewish brothers and sisters might wish to reciprocate by joining Muslims in a fast on Ashura. These are the sorts of practical religious acts that can create spiritual solidarity between people of different faiths.

I once fasted the nonobligatory fast of the middle of the month of Sha'ban; that year it happened to coincide with Christmas Day. In the Quran story about Jesus' conception and birth (described in chapter 19, called "Mary"), God commands Mary to fast the day she gives birth to Jesus. Because I knew that, I felt a special connection that day to Mary and Jesus, although I had fasted on mid-Sha'ban day several times before. It was a wonderful feeling. By understanding—and acting on—more of our history, and this inner *sunna* or attitude of the prophets to and between each other as brothers, we can foster and strengthen the sentiment that followers of all of the prophets are religious cousins.

It may come as a surprise to many of our Abrahamic brothers and sisters that the Hebrew prophets are significant figures in the Quran, an indispensable part of our tradition. Moses is especially noteworthy; he is mentioned by name in the Quran more frequently (136 times) than Muhammad (4 times). The Quran tells his story repeatedly, and Muslims discuss it frequently. For us too he confronted Pharaoh, led the Children of Israel out of Egypt, received the tablets from God, and was betrayed by the faithless while on Mount Sinai, all of which lessons are relevant to Muslim societies today.

For Muslims five prophets—Abraham, Noah, Moses, Jesus, and Muhammad—have particularly exalted status and are known as *uli l'azm*, or "messengers of inflexible purpose." But Muslims also embrace Isaac, Jacob, Aaron, Solomon, and David, among many other biblical prophets. Here is the key: just as Christians and Jews do not consider Solomon or David—or even Abraham, Moses, or Jesus, or any of the prophets—as having started their own religion, the Quran does not consider Moses, Jesus, and Muhammad as founders of separate religions. They were all God's messengers, believers in God, calling our ancestors, all of us, and future generations of humanity back to belief in the one God. After their deaths, their followers eventually created sects that became known as Judaism, Christianity, and Islam, and after generations, sects were created within each of these "religions" as well.

These three separate faiths have distinct (if often overlapping) histories, scriptures, practices, and liturgies, but from the divine point of view they tell the same story: that of God's religion. God is less interested in the Hebrew or Greek or Arabic word for "God" than whether humans accept Him and worship Him above all others, with whatever name they choose. During the Prophet's time, two men argued over whether they should address the Creator as Allah (God) or as ar-Rahman (the Compassionate or Merciful). Their dispute precipitated another Quranic revelation (revelations were often precipitated by events), in which God instructs the Prophet, "Say, call upon God or call upon The Compassionate; whichever you call upon, to Him belong the Beautiful Names" (Quran 17:110).

Just as adherents to the multiplicity of Protestant denominations and Roman Catholicism are all Christians, and Orthodox, Conservative, Reform, and Reconstructionist Jews are all Jews, and Sunni and Shia Muslims are all Muslims, what unites all of them is that they are believers in one God. That is the single most important and defining attribute of believers, says God in the Quran: that they fulfill and perform the First Commandment. What we think about God, as important as that is, is far less important than loving God, worshipping God, and devoting ourselves to God's service.

Rumi tells a funny story about this first point in "Moses and the Shepherd." He describes Moses in his travels passing by a shepherd who is in ecstasy about his feelings toward God. Moses overhears him gushing, "I want to help you, to fix your shoes and comb your hair. I want to wash your clothes and pick the lice off" and so on. Scandalized by such ridiculous descriptions of God, implying that God could have lice or dirty feet, Moses takes the man to task and upbraids him for his blasphemy. Later God takes Moses to task, saying that this servant of his was describing his love of God in his own limited understanding, and that God accepted his expressions of love, not for their accuracy but out of the depth of his longing and desire to serve Him. The story has a happy ending, though, for when Moses goes back to the shepherd to apologize, the shepherd thanks Moses profusely, for Moses' intervention launched the shepherd into a new level of spiritual advancement, as an intervention by a prophet always does.

Is God as interested in the distinctions between Sunni and Shia, Catholic and Protestant, Reform and Conservative, and other human-made religious distinctions, as we are? The Quran (23:52–53) quotes God telling His messengers, including Moses and Jesus, "Surely this your community [of believers] is one community, and I am your Lord; so keep your duty to Me. But they became divided into sects, with each group reveling in what differentiates them." Why, then, should human beings be so attached to these very differences—all in the name of God? For more than a thousand years adherents of these different religions have distinguished themselves from each other and have interacted a great deal with one another—both generously and horribly.

Abrahamic Faiths:
The Common Origins of Judaism, Christianity, and Islam

We Muslims trace our origins all the way back to Adam and Eve, as do Jews and Christians. Why? Because the Quran confirms the narratives of the Torah (the first five books of the Hebrew Bible) as divine scriptures: God literally speaking to humankind. The central biblical figure for Muslims is Abraham, the patriarch of monotheism, the belief in one god. Abraham distinguished himself in several ways. In the Quran he is depicted as seeking God. He refused to worship the idols that flourished among tribes and societies in the ancient Near East. Rejecting such gods, as well as his father, an idol maker, he asks his father, "How can you worship what you fabricate?" (Quran 37:95). Abraham first sought God in what other people worshipped, such as the sun, stars, and moon, but found it unsatisfying putting his faith in that which set or waned when he was seeking permanence, the Absolute Reality that creates. His search for God and divine grace was rewarded when God "unveiled" His existence to him, and he received the name *khalil-allah*, "friend of God." To me, Abraham's search and journey serves as a model for the general human search for God.

Equally important for Muslims, Abraham was the father of Ishmael, whom he sired with his servant Hagar, and then of Isaac, whom he sired with his wife Sarah. Through these two sons, he was the father of two extraordinary lines of prophets and messengers. The Prophet Muhammad was a descendant of Ishmael, while Jacob, Moses, Aaron, Solomon, David, and Jesus were all descendants of Isaac.

The story of Abraham and the prophets who came after him is about the human effort to develop a community of people who will adhere to God's religion. What is God's intent for us today? How do we interpret the Divine Imperative in the here and now? Prophets play key roles in this story because they come at moments of challenge, trial, and calamity, and our Prophet taught us that scholars are the inheritors of the prophets. So what should, and do, we do? The stories of the Children of Israel are told so often in the Quran because they describe the challenges of establishing and maintaining a believing community—challenges that befall every faith community and continue to challenge us today. The stories of the prophets are not just past history: they speak to the perennial human condition. This is what I seek to do in my sermons and work.

Think of what Moses faced, from Pharaoh to the Red Sea to his own anger, starvation, and betrayal. All of the prophets and their people had to face the problems of individual and collective evil, of powerful rulers and rivals, and their tendency to be drawn to the glitter and sinfulness of other societies—what we might call, metaphorically, the attractions of Egypt. Even after their liberation from slavery and the parting of the Red Sea, the Israelites forced Aaron—Moses' brother, no less—to make a golden calf as an object of worship. That story continues to this day, of course. We may not literally worship a golden calf; instead we worship wealth, celebrity (and sometimes celebrities themselves), our jobs, our cars, our houses, our own talents. Even ostensible monotheists, the Quran says, may be guilty of *shirk,* setting up false gods next to God.

For Christians, these attractions may be thought of as the behavior represented by the Seven Deadly Sins: anger, greed, sloth, pride, lust, envy, and gluttony. Sufi Muslims call these the diseases of the soul (or of the heart), the most virulent of which is pride or egotism.

We Muslims *should* feel enormous kinship with Jews and Christians, partly because we *are* kin—literal siblings in the great monotheistic adventure that began in the ancient Near East several thousand years ago. But also, in our holy book, the Quran, God speaks frequently about the "People of the Book"—Jews and Christians—whom we are taught to consider our brothers and sisters. Of course that does not mean that all of us think in such ways; many Muslims do not even regard fellow Muslims as spiritual brothers and sisters, much less Jews and Christians. But by seeing them as kin, we are able to also learn from their lessons and experiences and God's critiques. For example, God criticizes Jews in Quran 62:5–6 for thinking they are God's favorites to the exclusion of others; He says that those who were charged with the Torah and do not observe its commandments are like a donkey carrying books on its back. Because Jews are our predecessors, I see these verses as very applicable to contemporary Muslims. In my sermons I ask my listeners how many Muslims they know who behave as though they are God's favorites to the exclusion of others (even other Muslims). And aren't Muslims who haven't yet assimilated the Quranic teachings—while believing themselves to be passionately Muslim—no better than a donkey carrying the Quran on its back?

Jews emphasize the stories of Abraham and Isaac, Hagar, Sarah, and Ishmael. We tell the stories a little differently. In the Jewish understanding of the "binding of Isaac," for example, Abraham is on the verge of sacrificing his son Isaac when an angel intervenes and points out a ram to sacrifice instead. In the Muslim narrative, Abraham is about to sacrifice Ishmael when the angel intervenes by offering Abraham a ram instead. Later, God rewards Abraham with another son, Isaac, for having passed this test. In the Bible, the banishment of Hagar and Ishmael has a happy result, since God both provides a well for them in the desert and promises Abraham that Ishmael will found a nation. For Muslims, the story is foundational, for the nation predicted is that of the Prophet Muhammad and his followers. God saved the lives of Hagar and Ishmael by providing water in the desert, in the form of a well called Zamzam. Some years later Abraham returned to the site, and together with Ishmael built the original mosque, the first structure dedicated to the worship of the one God: the Kaaba. This cubical structure built of stone and covered with a black shroud remains the holiest site in Islam and was the reason for founding Mecca itself.

Abraham began the practice of an annual pilgrimage to Mecca, and today Muslims undertaking the *hajj* reenact Hagar's desperate search for water. We run back and forth between the same two hills as she did, and circle the Kaaba ritualistically. Many kiss the stone, the cornerstone of which is said to have come from heaven and to have been laid by Abraham himself. At the conclusion of the *hajj* Muslims reenact Abraham's gratitude by sacrificing a lamb or a sheep and feeding it to the poor. As you can see, one of the most famous traditions of Islam, a pillar of our faith, comes directly from shared Abrahamic traditions.

Islam sees itself connected to Abraham, and so did the Prophet Muhammad, who said that physically he most resembled Abraham among the prophets; in our five-times-daily prayers we ask God to invoke His blessings upon Muhammad and add, "as You have invoked Your blessings upon Abraham." We mention Abraham's name in these daily prayers a minimum of twenty times and as many as sixty.

However, we Muslims do not stop with the Torah. We consider Jesus and the Christian Gospels part of our religious heritage as well. The Quran (3:42) prefaces the story of angels announcing to Mary that she would bear a son, Jesus, who would be known as the Messiah, with the declaration, "He has chosen thee above all women." Mary is therefore considered by Muslims as the best, the most godly of women. Some Muslims rank her as a prophet, because in addition to her purity she received a direct revelation from God.

A messenger is a prophet who is given the additional mandate to preach. As God says, "We indeed gave Moses the Book, and sent a string of messengers succeeding him, and We gave Jesus son of Mary clear arguments, aiding him with the Holy Spirit" (Quran 2:87). For

Muslims, Jesus was the greatest messenger immediately before Muhammad himself. There are twenty-five references to Jesus by name in the Quran, and many more in *hadith*s and related Muslim stories. Like every prophet, Jesus came to recalibrate and teach God's religion and to bring believers back to the First Commandment. And like other Jewish prophets before him—such as Jeremiah, Isaiah, and Ezekiel—Jesus subjected the Jewish religious, legal, and political establishment of the day to powerful, withering criticism from within.

But the greatest aspect of Jesus' mission, his signature, was to be a conveyor of the most powerful spirituality and connection to God; by accessing "God's permission" (*idhn*) he performed miracles. The Sufis regard Jesus as the Master of all Sufis, who taught his disciples how to access the power of the Holy Spirit and be instruments of God's beauty and Will.

For Muslims, all prophets prior to Muhammad came with their own "signatures." Joseph, for instance, was an interpreter of dreams and signs; Moses, a lawgiver; David and Solomon were kings; Jesus came with powerful spirituality. The Prophet Muhammad was the final expression of prophethood, embracing, including, and summarizing the qualities of all previous prophets; thus he interpreted dreams, brought law, served as ruler, and channeled a faith that embodies a powerful spirituality.

Islam and Non-Abrahamic Religions

Muslims believe, as the Quran (10:47) says, that God "raised in every nation a messenger," or representative, of God to speak to the people in "their own language." However, "some [of these messengers] We have named, and some We have not named" (Quran 4:64). There are three critical points here. First, God sent messengers throughout the world: to India, China, Africa, Europe, to indigenous peoples everywhere. Second, these messengers spread God's religion to people in their language and in their own cultural traditions. Even if they did not speak Arabic or Aramaic, Hebrew or any Middle Eastern language, they could hear the word of God. Third, although we do know the names of the Abrahamic messengers, the others we do not know by name at all.

For example, in India Muslims have lived adjacent to Hindus for a millennium, and Indian Muslims developed a theology that regarded Hindus—by virtue of the above argument—as an extension of People of the Book. In China Muslims have considered Buddha, Confucius, and Lao Tzu to be prophets; thus many Muslims treat Buddhists too as People of the Book. So even though the Quran does not explicitly refer to Hindu, Buddhist, Confucian, Jain, Shinto, Zoroastrian, or Taoist religious practice, we must acknowledge that all of these adherents had to have prophets who taught them to practice in this way, and we Muslims are obliged to honor the practitioners of these faiths.

More than a thousand years ago this was a breathtaking understanding and endorsement of religious diversity; it remains even more remarkable today, especially as we know more about geography. We now know of North and South America and of Australia, areas of the world unknown to peoples living in Mecca and Medina at the time of the Prophet. How many Muslims *actually believe* that God sent prophets to these regions, to the Aztecs, the Mayans, the Native American Indians, and the Australian Aborigines, even though God explicitly says He did?

How many adherents of the world's major religions even now, in the twenty-first century, would feel comfortable, much less eager, saying, in effect, "God established paths to the divine in different languages and different liturgies—and on all continents"? That not enough of us express such beliefs loudly and insistently is one reason extremists have achieved strong footholds in all the major religions. Almost by definition, they seize on the parts of any religion that distinguish it most fully from others, rather than seeking the far larger areas of agreement that exist among many, if not all, of the world's major religions.

Despite these exceptionally clear words in the Quran, and the fact that to be a Muslim you have to believe the teachings of the Quran, more and more Muslims in the past fifty years have treated members of other faith traditions with hostility rather than with this understanding of kinship. How could it be to the greater glory of God to prohibit Jews or Christians from worshipping God, when God Himself says that he gave other religions "rites which they perform" (Quran 22:67)? This practice of prohibiting other Peoples of the Book from worshipping invokes the worst features of Inquisition-like religion, directly contradicts God's own commandments, and therefore ought to be rejected by all Muslims everywhere, *especially* in countries where Muslims hold political and religious power. As I pointed out earlier, Quranic teachings not only require intellectual understanding; they imply the need for action as well. In a well-known story, a young man asked the Prophet's wife Aisha what the Prophet was like. She answered, "His character was the Quran" (Ibn Hanbal 25873). Assimilating teachings into behavior is the work we Muslims have to do to become more like the Prophet.

Islam and Atheism

As far as the Quran and the *hadith*s are concerned, Muslims have no problem coexisting with atheists. None. Even though disbelief is the one unforgivable sin, punished by God in the hereafter, the Quran authorizes no worldly authority to punish another for not believing in or worshipping God. That is between the individual and God on Judgment Day. Choosing God has to be a free human choice to be valid at all.

The historical (as opposed to theological) problem posed by organized atheism has been much more important, mainly because of its association with Communism. Militant Communism caused enormous troubles in the Muslim world. The Soviet Union tried hard to bring Communism to newly independent Muslim countries, such as

Yemen, Egypt, Indonesia, and Afghanistan, in the latter half of the twentieth century. The eventual backlash against these efforts led to the rise of extremist Muslim fundamentalism in all of these countries.

The reactions in Afghanistan had particularly far-reaching repercussions, as the United States funded and trained Muslim mujahedeen to fight against the Soviet occupation, helping build the Taliban and the career and reputation of America's greatest nemesis, Osama bin Laden, and America's longest war.

Since there seems to be a newly militant, if unorganized, atheism afoot, as signaled in bestsellers by the late Christopher Hitchens and Richard Dawkins, among others, it seems important to address this phenomenon, which seems to me an unfortunate if understandable reaction to religious extremists of all types.

Extremist atheists do what extremist believers do: they point to the most barbaric and punitive practices of religious zealots and suggest that they stand for all believers and that their practices stand for all religions. Then they either mock or scorn these bizarre concoctions, which is both unfair and a logical fallacy. The Taliban during the 1990s made a perfect foil, since they were thuggish *and* hypocritical extremists; so do high-flying male Christian evangelical ministers who exalt "family values" and preach fire and brimstone sermons about homosexuality, while secretly soliciting male prostitutes on business trips.

But militant atheists rarely take religion seriously enough to investigate and grapple with open, joyful, intellectually and theologically sophisticated religion. Nor do they engage the great Christian and Jewish activists who articulated a vision of social justice that has helped sustain movements for peace and racial and economic justice in the past 150 years of American history. Many atheists think they have stumped believers by asking the question, "If God is all-powerful, then why is there evil in the world?" Yet why assume that religions dating back thousands of years could have somehow "missed" this question, instead of struggling with it for centuries and developing a theology of evil? Atheists imply that believers must have checked their intelligence at the door of the synagogue, mosque, or church. Most of us in the Abrahamic traditions believe that God created humankind to be free to do good and evil. Why? Because the concepts of good and evil have no meaning if there is no human choice.

There is a story in the beginning of the Quran, in which God assembles the angels and tells them that He is going to create a successor (a vice regent), that is, human beings. The angels are shocked by this move; they point out to God that humans are simply going to shed blood and create mischief. God replies, "I know that which you do not"; in other words, God knew very well that we would commit evil acts (Quran 2:30). In our theology, God's knowledge that human beings would commit evil predated their creation. This is because God wanted to create a being that was as like God as possible: *a being created in the divine image*. God says in the Quran that if there were multiple gods other than God in the universe, there would be chaos, suggesting that the gods would be fighting among themselves, as happens among the Greek pantheon of gods. And because we are created in the divine image, God gave us a region of the universe, Earth, in which we can, and do, act like gods, fighting each other for dominion and acquiring learning and inventing technology that amplifies our ability to destroy and kill, so much so that now we can destroy the Earth itself.

But there is a larger purpose to all this. God's aspiration for us is to truly surrender to Him and become godly like the prophets; if not, we act like gods and make a mess of things. Even when confronted with God's power in the ten plagues, Pharaoh refused until the very end to recognize that there was a being more powerful than he. Modern dictators too imagine themselves as God (whether or not they use the language) and commit evil on an unimaginable scale: consider Hitler, Stalin, Pol Pot, Idi Amin, Mobutu Sese Seko, Saddam Hussein.

But evil is not only individual. The real evil represented by Soviet Communist atheism was its character as a proselytizing ideology with the political, economic, and military power of a nation-state behind it. At their best, Western countries have figured out that humanity needs protection from any proselytizing ideology that is willing to force particular beliefs on other people. Whether it is atheism in the Soviet Communist world, or the Taliban's Muslim fundamentalism ruling Afghanistan in the 1990s, or the Holy Roman Empire, or the Spanish Inquisition—*any country that forces on people one religion or one interpretation of a religion, backed by state power, and destroys human free will, is the true danger to us all.* This is a principle that can and should unite Jews, Christians, Muslims, all peoples of all faiths—and atheists—around the world.

Since organized, militant atheism (in the form of Communism) has had truly dreadful consequences in the world, I am less worried about the bestseller list. I *am* concerned about the mocking and dismissive tone of these books, because they poison the possibility of discourse between people who desperately need to understand each other: moderates of all faiths as well as atheists. You do not make someone give up an idea or a position by ridiculing him or his ideas. On the contrary, you strengthen his attachment to his beliefs and convince him that you can never be trusted to have a conversation.

Muslims can and do, however, live with and befriend atheists who believe and practice the Golden Rule, who refrain from treating people in ways they themselves would not like to be treated. I believe therefore that a harmonious and just society is one that allows and encourages people to believe what they want to with respect to God. (They will anyway, and whether people obey the First Commandment is up to them and up to God.) More important, a harmonious and just society is one that, while it encourages people to recognize and love God, universally applies the Second Commandment.

Religion After 9/11

On September 10, 2001, I conducted my daughter Amira's wedding in Golden, Colorado, on the outskirts of Denver. The next morning, as Daisy and I were enjoying a leisurely breakfast, the television in the hotel dining room suddenly began showing footage of the Twin Towers spewing smoke and flames. We rushed closer and then stayed riveted to the TV as the horrible events unfolded with dreamlike clarity. These were buildings in our city, just blocks from our mosque—this cityscape we saw every day had become a scene of unimaginable horror, played over and over in an endless loop. We felt terrible about all the people dying, burning, crushed, falling to their deaths. We worried about the mosque and what would happen to it, just blocks from the World Trade Center. What would happen to the city? By now we knew about the Pentagon too. What else would come under attack? We could not reach anyone in New York: cell phone service had crashed.

In the days after the catastrophe, as it became clear that radical Muslims had carried out the attacks, our hearts sank. I knew that extremism was growing, that Samuel Huntington's predictions were coming true, like a self-fulfilling prophecy. At the same time, I knew that most of the world's Muslims shared American Muslims' horror and sadness at this vicious and un-Islamic attack on innocent people in a great nation. I feared that the American Muslim community was headed for some dark days.

But Americans are not prisoners of their worst instincts. Just as Jews reached out to my father in the aftermath of the Six-Day War, Americans of different faiths reached out to me following the September 11 attacks. Shortly after the catastrophe, Americans wanted—and needed—most to hear from Muslims. That's why I and many other Muslims were inundated with requests to speak at churches, synagogues, businesses, schools, even Kiwanis and Rotary Clubs, to explain Islam, to shed light on who the extremists were and what was going on with "Islam versus the West." As odd as it may seem, in times of crisis people have a visceral, powerful need to reach out across the boundaries we see as dividing us in "normal times."

I remember giving a talk at a church in Westchester County a month or two after 9/11. I began with my usual fifteen-minute introduction to Islam's creed and practice before getting to questions. In this case, the questions went on for much longer than the scheduled hour; in fact they continued for almost three hours. No more than three or four people out of the 100 to 150 in attendance left the hall the entire time.

All of these talks right after 9/11 were very intense experiences. At first, people often had feelings of hurt and anger, even rage. But once they'd expressed their emotions, gotten them off their chest, they often thanked Muslim speakers like me for allowing them to speak out. Imagine that: they felt grateful to the representatives of the faith by which they felt attacked! Giving them the opportunity to say whatever was on their mind and answering as honestly as I could showed me that we Americans want honest engagement, and that when we are honest with each other and try hard to engage, the response is very positive.

This is why I say to people in the Muslim world that most Americans want a better relationship with Muslims. That surprises many of them, but it is the truth. It is equally true—I know it based on a lifetime of experience—that in the Muslim world, most Muslims want a better relationship with America.

In 2004 I published my book *What's Right with Islam,* partly to set the record straight about the Islam I know and love. My first major interview was with Paula Zahn on CNN. My family and friends were thrilled to see me on TV. I had been trained by specialists to stay on message, to remain calm, and to smile. But no amount of preparation could have prepared me for what happened in the interview. Zahn introduced me as the imam who has written "this wonderful book" called *What's Right with Islam.* But there had been a news flash: Muslim extremists had beheaded Nick Berg, a young American contractor in Iraq. She ran the tape of his beheading and then asked me, "Why would they do that?" I have no idea what I said.

I felt sick to my stomach and was deeply saddened for that poor man, his family, for my faith and my people. And I was in trouble.

I had written a book called *What's Right with Islam,* and here I was watching an example of all that was wrong with Islam.

In 2003, when I was writing the book, I was invited by Rabbi Rolando Matalon to speak at the New York memorial service for the Jewish journalist Daniel Pearl, murdered by Muslim extremists the previous year. I felt it was my duty to stand at a podium at the Upper West Side synagogue B'Nai Jeshurun and to address my words to Judea Pearl, Daniel's father. To him and all who were present, I said what I felt needed to be said on behalf of all God-fearing Muslims, who I knew shared the following belief:

> If to be a Jew means to say with all one's heart, mind and soul "Shema Yisrael, Adonai Elohenu, Adonai Echad"—Hear O Israel, the Lord our God, the Lord is One—not only today am I a Jew, but I have always been one, Mr. Pearl.
>
> If to be a Christian is to love the Lord our God with all of my heart, mind and soul, and to love for my fellow human being what I love for myself, then not only am I a Christian, but I have always been one, Mr. Pearl.
>
> And I am here to inform you, with the full authority of the Quranic texts and the practice of the Prophet Muhammad, that to say, *La ilaha illallah Muhammadun rasulullah*—I bear witness that there is no god but God, and I bear witness that Muhammad is God's Messenger—is no different.

Seven years later, in August 2010, in the middle of the Cordoba House crisis, New York City's mayor Michael Bloomberg gave a speech at Gracie Mansion marking the month of Ramadan. Much to my surprise, he cited these very words of mine, and according to Daisy, who was in the audience, he choked up. This is the power of genuine interfaith connection, one made possible by human beings of goodwill and the fundamental similarities of our religious beliefs. Mayor Bloomberg is not known as a sentimental man. Nevertheless he showed what can happen when we take each other's religion seriously. Here he was, the Jewish mayor of New York, the city with the largest Jewish population in the world, during Ramadan, quoting me, a Muslim, reciting his own Hebrew prayer, the Shema—admittedly, not just any prayer: it is the foundational prayer of Judaism—and *he* got choked up.

The theological and historical connections between the three Abrahamic faiths do not, I realize, address the very real conflicts between, say, Hindus and Muslims in India, or between India and Pakistan over Kashmir. But even those deep-seated, occasionally bloody rivalries have less to do with religion than with politics, culture, and the history of colonialism and nationalism. We know that one of the most successful British colonial tactics was to foment divisions between tribes in Africa and castes and religious groupings in India.

There is nothing easy about unlearning generations of competition, mutual fear and suspicion, and now a history of horrifying, graphic, violent grievances that are endlessly recycled through popular culture. But people have to start by sitting with each other, befriending each other, and trusting each other. Out of friendships we learn about each other and realize that much of the hatred in our communities is the result of political machinations. If we Muslims—and all believers of all faiths—go to the touchstones of our faith and surrender to God and God's holy word, we can learn from His command "Be not divided therein." The future of our world depends on it.

4
THE MODERN AMERICAN MUSLIM WOMAN

The Prophet as Feminist

The modern Muslim woman, perhaps especially in America, is the heir to a tradition of cultural strength and fundamental legal and religious rights. The Prophet Muhammad brought enormous changes for women and to their status, explicitly and implicitly—so much so that I consider him an early women's liberationist, remarkable for his time. His respect for women resonates down through the ages without the need for setting the cultural context. But when we understand the context, his intervention in history becomes all the more striking and powerful.

At the time of the Prophet, women were the legal property of men in the Arabian Peninsula, but also throughout the rest of the Middle East and in Europe, China, and Africa. Generally men could marry as many women as they wished, and women had virtually no property or inheritance rights. The Prophet determined that women could no longer be disinherited (neither could men). According to the Quran, women were entitled to half of their brothers' equal shares. This difference was a simple matter of logic: since women were not required to support families, while men were, men received larger shares. The Quran established a limit to the number of wives a man could have (four); there had been no limit before. Male followers of the Prophet who had more than four wives had to divorce enough of them to get down to four. Just as important, if not more so, the Quran contains the truly radical notion that men were now required to treat all their wives equally in time, attention, and material gifts and property, notwithstanding how unequal they might feel emotionally toward them. This was contrary to previous custom (and customs throughout the world), in which wives' seniority or illness or mishaps, and husbands' whims, could lead to their unequal treatment.

I know that today few would argue that polygamy represents a form of women's liberation. But in the context of the Prophet's own times, he and the Quran made what can only be considered revolutionary changes in the status of women.

The more we study his life, the clearer it becomes that the success of the Prophet's mission to bring human beings to God (which is every prophet's primary objective) was due in no small degree to the women who believed in him.

The Prophet married his first wife, Khadijah, when he was twenty-five and she was roughly forty—fifteen years older. A very well-known and wealthy woman, whom many men had sought to marry, she had employed Muhammad as a young man, found herself impressed by his trustworthiness, honesty, and skill, fell in love with him, and proposed marriage. He accepted her proposal and stayed married to her—monogamously, at a time when men commonly married multiple wives—until she died about twenty-five years later, after a deeply loving marriage.

It was during their marriage that the Prophet received his first revelations from the Angel Jibril, which was an experience neither were prepared for; both found it difficult to process. Muhammad was perplexed and shocked and felt helpless as he grappled with this unexpected divine intervention. (Even the great prophet Moses, remember, tried to avoid God's intervention in his life no fewer than four times!) It was Khadijah who assuaged Muhammad's fears, walked him through his periods of doubt, and played a vital role in helping him psychologically during this tumultuous period of transformation.

Khadijah had such complete and implicit trust in her husband that she never doubted that God had chosen him as His Messenger. She was the first person to accept the Prophet's message and supported his prophecy until her death. She was and remains a key figure in the history of Islam; even today many Muslim parents name their daughters for this remarkable woman.

Consider the challenge Khadijah faced, as the man she married became God's last Messenger to humanity, one of the most significant men in human history! A marriage, even a strong marriage between relative equals, requires a delicate balancing of needs and desires in order to remain successful over time. Imagine the effect on a marriage when one of the partners begins to receive divine revelations. There are women who would have been psychologically overwhelmed by this transformation; women who would have resented the burden or costs incurred by being the wife of a prophet; and women who would have run from their new responsibilities. According to the Quran, the wives of the prophets Noah and Lot both rejected their respective husbands' status as prophets.

At the core of Islam, then, even before the birth of the religion, there was a powerful, self-aware woman of skill and intelligence and spirit who had a long marriage with the Messenger, the most important man in Muslim history. And at the birth of Islam was a man, the Prophet Muhammad, who loved and respected a strong and capable woman substantially older than he was, who was clearly looking for something deeper in a wife than youthful appearance.

Women other than Khadijah played key roles at critical moments in the development of the faith. Caliph Umar's conversion to Islam, for instance, had much to do with his sister Fatima. It is quite a story. She and her husband accepted Islam early. Umar, however, infuriated at how the Prophet's mission was dividing Meccan society, decided to kill him. En route to accomplish the deed, he ran into his best friend, who told him his own sister Fatima and her husband had both become Muslims, so Umar went to their house first. While her husband hid out of fear (Umar was a physically powerful man), Umar turned on his sister and gave her a serious beating. Fatima, however, maintained her pride and dignity in the face of this brutality, declaring, "You may kill us if you like, but we will not waver in our faith." Umar felt deep remorse for his actions, and he asked to hear some of the Quran's verses that Fatima and her husband had been reciting. Upon hearing them he was transformed. Umar, regarded as one of the most influential people in Islamic history, was converted by the actions and faith commitment of a woman, his sister.

The Prophet consistently encouraged spiritual growth and social strength in the women around him. In the first battles on behalf of the believing community, women accompanied male warriors, to fight, to encourage and prod their warriors, and to nurse the wounded. These battles could not have been won without the vital support of women.

Widowed at about the age of fifty, only then did the Prophet marry again. As was often the case in ancient times, he married for political reasons: to take care of a widow, say, or to strengthen his bond with certain key leaders. In purely religious terms, the Prophet's wives were major sources for many of the *hadith*s. They contributed to a vast body of knowledge about the Prophet's personal life, how he worshipped and made decisions, their own role in helping him make decisions, and his transformative power with respect to other people. They gave us another lens through which to view the Prophet and his example, and thereby contributed greatly to Muslim learning. They were teachers and instructors in the faith, helped explain Quranic verses, and contributed to the *Hadith*. Muhammad's youngest wife, Aisha, who lived for many decades after the Prophet's death, is an especially important figure in Islamic history and law for just that reason. The second-generation Muslims (those too young to have known the Prophet while he was alive or who were born after his death) frequently came to her and asked if certain practices were requirements. She gave significant rulings based on the Prophet's practice.

How dreadful it is, then, that in so many Muslim countries women's status has eroded from the Prophet's time. It is undeniable that in many Muslim countries around the world, women's rights and opportunities are far more restricted than in Western countries. In fact, according to the World Economic Forum, twenty of the twenty-five "worst" countries in the world for women's participation in society have Muslim majorities. On the other hand—and it is a very large other hand—*American* Muslim women have higher educational levels than the average American and are better educated even than Western European women. The gap between American Muslim men's and women's income is smaller than for any other religious grouping in America.

I think we need to pause and consider the achievements of Muslim women in our country. They have fully grasped the opportunities available to them. They have not walked behind their men, remaining subject to ancient patriarchal systems widespread in the developing world. They are attending college, improving their employment opportunities, attending mosques, and being civically engaged, all the while remaining proud Muslims in the face of a popular culture that is often condescending at best and hostile and violent at worst.

Our Duty in Advocating for Women's Rights

Is it fair to attribute the strength and vitality of American Muslim women to an ancient faith born in seventh-century Arabia? I believe so. Bearing witness to Muhammad as the Messenger of God means that we self-consciously model our own practice on the Prophet's, which I—and millions of today's Muslims—do deliberatively and purposefully. Given the Prophet's revolutionary intervention in the structure of gender relations, Muslims today need to maintain the Prophet's groundbreaking desire to continually improve the status of women. This argument raises important questions about Islamic law and Quranic interpretation.

The Prophet's pronouncements, and the Quran's, by moving in the *direction* of an egalitarian society, pointed the way toward a genuinely different status for women. The real questions about God's intent regarding gender relations as revealed in the Quran and as articulated by the Prophet are these: Is the proper benchmark what the Prophet achieved in his societal context in his lifetime? Or is the benchmark *his striving* to achieve gender parity and justice?

If it is the first, then the status the Prophet achieved for women in seventh-century Arabia becomes our norm—and some Muslims do insist on this. If the answer is the second, then we have to strive to do what the Prophet did for seventh-century Arabia in the context of twenty-first-century America. That is, if the Prophet were alive today in America—and imagine that his independently wealthy wife Khadijah was by his side—would either of them be satisfied that the status of women in America be that of women's status in seventh-century Arabia? Muslim legal scholars have always tried to understand divine intent and apply it to their own social contexts. And this is what we have to do in America.

Thus retired chief justice of Malaysia Tun Abdul Hamid Mohamed argues that when divine intent is clear, not only is it possible, *it is mandatory* for contemporary societies to enact laws that strive to improve the on-the-ground reality beyond what the Prophet Muhammad may have achieved in his society during his lifetime.

As an example, Hamid cites slavery, widespread at the Prophet's time. Throughout the twenty-two-year period of God's revelations constituting the Quran, God encourages freeing of the slaves (Quran 2:177, 90:13), to the point of mandating that if a slave requested his freedom, the owner not only had to give him the option to purchase it, but even provide him with the money to do so and enable him to start his life as a free man (Quran 24:33). So while the Quran is unequivocal on the equality of men and encourages freeing slaves—to the point that it is clear that it frowns on slavery—it did not prohibit slavery outright. So, my friend Tun Hamid asks, if Medina at the Prophet's time represents the ideal and very best Muslim society, which many Muslims believe, should we reinstitute slavery in our communities to better resemble the (mythically ideal) reality at time of the Prophet? After all, slavery is outlawed today all over the world.

No contemporary Islamic scholar, not even the most extreme fundamentalist he has asked, has ever answered affirmatively. Thus, he argues by analogy (a source of Islamic law), if it is clear from the Quran and the Prophet's practice that gender equality is an Islamic principle, and if during the twenty-two-year period of the Prophet he did much to improve the status of women but did not achieve complete gender equality, our obligation in the twenty-first century must be to further what the Prophet achieved in his lifetime.

That is why I believe Muslims' task today is to bring the Quranic intent to fruition, to move *forward* toward ideal and complete justice appropriate to our time and context—and not to go backward and re-institutionalize social arrangements appropriate to a society more than a thousand years old. Reality has a way of nudging us forward, and the reality today is that gender equality is a growing aspect of Muslim society.

Muslim Women in America—and Abroad

My hope for American Muslim women is that they will step further into the limelight, transforming the images non-Muslims have of Muslim women around the world. The more forcefully they speak in mixed company, the more they will destroy the stereotypes of Muslim women as quiet, repressed appendages to men. American Muslim women are already shattering stereotypes in this country, but because of what they are doing here, and because of the importance of America to the rest of the world, they are effecting change on a global level.

The key for American Muslim women, I believe, is to more robustly claim their new status in our country: in business, law, politics, government, health care, education, sports, and entertainment. It seems to be a relatively consistent pattern in the lives of immigrants that the first generation tends to be more cautious, more anxious to live under the radar, as it were, hoping to escape the notice and derision of native-born Americans. It tends to be the second generation—speaking unaccented English, learning American culture from television at a young age—that steps out of the immigrant cultural framework and into the larger society.

Those of us who hold religious authority have an obligation to educate our coreligionists about women's place both in Islam and in American society. In the Prophet's time, for example, women were expected to be carrying out family obligations, so while they were required to pray, they were not required, as men were, to attend the weekly Friday prayers in the mosque. But as a younger generation of more educated women are increasingly choosing to be devoted to their faith, they are also choosing to attend Friday prayers, even though they are not required to attend. Yet in many mosques, women are still marginalized, made to worship in the basement during Friday prayers or in other separate, unpleasant, and restricted spaces. Oftentimes men react rudely and dismissively to their presence, grumbling, "They don't need to be here. We don't have enough space for ourselves."

Muslim women deserve to be treated as equals in the mosque, fully participating in the spiritual experience. As the primary educators of children, they need to have equal access to religious teachings. In my mosque, where I lead Friday prayers, I have insisted that women have their own separate, adequate space on the main floor, where they can see the imam and feel integrated into the main congregation. A separate space for women in prayer is not an absolute, however, as you will see men and women praying together in the Sacred Mosque in Mecca.

Even though the ideal of gender equality has a long way to go in many Muslim-majority countries, American stereotypes regarding Muslim women around the world are often mistaken. Because there has been so much attention paid to the issue of women not being allowed to drive in Saudi Arabia, some have come to think that the Muslim world is monolithic on this score, when the fact is that Saudi Arabia is the *only* country in the Muslim world where women are not allowed to drive. All over the Muslim world women drive cars, and in Southeast Asia especially they drive scooters.

My Egyptian-born and -raised mother remains, in her eighties, an extremely forceful and strong-willed woman. It felt completely natural for me as an Egyptian—and Egypt has an ancient history of queens like Nefertiti and Cleopatra—to be learning and practicing a religion committed to women's rights and equality. My mother would have tolerated nothing less!

There have been women prime ministers and presidents in the Muslim-majority countries of Indonesia, Pakistan, Turkey, Kosovo, Senegal, Kyrgyzstan, and Bangladesh, which has had two! How is it that non-Muslim Americans (and even some Muslims) casually assume the patriarchal nature of majority-Muslim countries, seven of which have had female heads of state while the United States awaits its first?

Take a minute and try to imagine a woman chair of the Federal Reserve, or a female secretary of the Treasury in the United States. Boggles the mind, doesn't it? Wall Street and finance are such male preserves in this country that picturing women in these roles is almost as difficult as imagining a female secretary of defense. And yet Malaysia has already had a female governor of its central bank, as well as a number of university presidents, and a woman, Sri Mulyani Indrawati, served as Indonesian finance minister from 2005 to 2010. As of this writing she is one of three managing directors at the World Bank in Washington, D.C.

Muslim women populate other traditionally male professions as well. There were women police officers in Malaysia as early as two decades ago. In fall 2010, even under the authoritarian Mubarak regime, the Egyptian Parliament set aside sixty-four seats for women, guaranteeing that women would make up about 12 percent of the new People's Assembly. By way of contrast, in the far more democratic United States, women made up just 16.5 percent of the Congress in 2011.

Women have had the right to own property in Egypt since antiquity (a right confirmed by Islam), long before they began to gain it in the United States. When I lived in Egypt, men and women earned the same salary for the same work. It was only when I arrived in the United States that I encountered women doing identical jobs as men and earning less!

At the American Society for Muslim Advancement my extraordinary wife, Daisy, runs the WISE Project, the Women's Islamic Initiative in Spirituality and Equality. Working from the theological and social justice premises I have laid out here, this project is helping to bring an orthodox, classical, Islamic perspective on the role of women, continuing the example of the Prophet—that women are the religious and social equals of men—to a wide range of cultural practices that have ignored or oppressed Muslim women around the world.

Daisy was giving a lecture at St. Bartholomew's Church in New York in 2002 when a woman in the audience stood up and fired a whole series of questions at her about women's place in Islam. One of those questions was why there were no female imams, which Daisy could not answer. So she came to me. The simplest answer is "tradition," but the truth is a little more complicated.

We do not have ordained clergy in Islam. People who ask why there are no female imams assume that the question is like asking "Why are there no female priests?" But it's not a precisely analogous question, since imams are not equivalent to priests. Here in America, in order to fit into the culture, we have created clerical positions—imams for mosques and chaplains for the military and hospitals—but those are clerical roles that do not come out of our tradition.

In the mosque an imam is a functionary, leading the prayers the way the muezzin calls the prayer. And since traditionally men have gone to the mosque for Friday prayers and women have not, men were appointed to be the imams. But that is not the end of the story, not by a long shot. As women attend mosques more and more and become regular Friday participants, they will raise the issue, and in time I believe there will be women imams. After all, the Prophet empowered a woman to lead her family in prayer; it makes sense that she could lead her community as well.

But the much more interesting and significant answer is that imams who lead congregational prayers are not the primary shapers of Islamic thought. Those with real influence are the scholars who issue fatwas (rulings) in Islamic law, something muftis (Islamic scholars and jurists, some of whom become judges) can do. There is no prohibition on women becoming muftis—the Arabic word is *muftiyyah* for women—and no reason women could not form their own Shura Council (a council of advisers, often in the form of a council of jurists) in order to effectuate real social change.

So it was that in 2006 Daisy set about organizing the first all-female Shura Council in Islamic history, consisting of a remarkable international group of female scholars, lawyers, journalists, historians, activists, and others prepared to issue religiously grounded opinions on matters of particular interest to Muslim women around the world. Currently these members of the Shura Council are also playing a key role in developing the first-ever *muftiyyah* curriculum (to be offered at the venerable Union Theological Seminary in New York), which will produce women graduates with a doctorate in Islamic law as well as the traditional certification, known as *Ijaaza al-Ilmiyyah.*

This is religiously groundbreaking, catalytic work whose time has come. The global reaction to the Council has been deeply gratifying. Syria soon appointed a *muftiyyah,* as did Abu Dhabi, while Egypt and Turkey appointed vice *muftiyyah*s. Palestine appointed two female Shariah judges, and King Abdullah of Saudi Arabia announced in October 2011 that women would be joining the nation's Shura Council in the next term. Would all of these developments have happened without our initiative based here in the United States? I cannot say for sure, but I like to think that the buzz we created catalyzed the global discourse, and the natural human competitive instinct kicked in. This is one example of why and how I believe American Muslims will play a major role in bringing change to the world. Islam is a global religion, and though there are culturally specific expressions of our faith, in an Internet-connected world there is no firewall between Muslims in Pakistan, Indonesia, China, Saudi Arabia, and the United States. While American Muslims can learn much from the rest of the Muslim world, what they do here can have a large, positive, transformative impact abroad as well.

From what we've learned in America about Afghanistan, there is a powerful misperception—certainly fostered by the Taliban, but having nothing to do with mainstream orthodox Islam—that women ought *not* to be educated. In fact there were frequent attacks on girls' schools by extremists in the years after the Taliban were deposed. Another initiative Daisy developed through the WISE Project was to educate imams in Afghanistan on women's rights. This included developing sermons, with citations from the Quran and the *Hadith,* that imams delivered in Kabul on women's rights to property and education and their right not to be forced into marriage against their will.

At one of these sermons one of our NGO partner organizations had sent a monitor who saw an older gentleman looking very distraught. "Uncle," he asked the man, "what is the matter? How can I help you?" "No one can help me," he answered in despair. "Why is that, uncle?" "Well, you know," he replied, "I did not educate my daughter, I consumed her dowry [which is the bride's property according to Shariah, not her father's, despite much common practice in the Muslim world], and I denied her her rights under Islamic law, and now it's too late for her and for me. Why didn't the imams tell me all this before?"

This story demonstrates how it is possible to change minds, to work against the cultural influences that have undermined the genuine, classical Muslim commitment to women's equality. Education is already making immense changes in the Muslim world. Even in Iran, not known in the West as a hotbed of women's rights, two-thirds of the university population is women, and a woman has served as vice president. Similar percentages of women attend universities throughout the Gulf states. It is no accident that Iranian women made up a very significant proportion of those demonstrating for more democratic government in Teheran in February 2011. Women were critical participants throughout the Middle East during the Arab uprising of 2011.

In the most traditional countries, like Saudi Arabia, growing numbers of fathers want a better future for their daughters. During our campaign for women's education, we heard from a former minister in Saudi Arabia, the equivalent of a cabinet secretary in the United States. He called Daisy and said, "I want to know everything about your initiative." "Why is that?" she asked. "You're a man." "You don't understand," he replied. "I have two daughters, and I want them to be empowered, to realize their full potential. I'm ready to help you on *their* behalf." And he did. He translated into Arabic an important paper produced by the Muslim Women's Shura Council titled "Jihad against Violence."

So even in a country as conservative as Saudi Arabia, we are seeing tectonic changes in gender relations. When King Abdullah announced that he would be appointing women to the Shura Council, he also announced that women would be able to vote and run for office in the next round of municipal elections. Given the importance of Saudi Arabia among Muslims worldwide, these decisions will have enormous influence throughout the Muslim world.

In 2001, shortly after 9/11, a friend of Daisy's and mine started a girls' school in Pakistan, whose teachers and management were routinely insulted by a local religious leader for being "un-Islamic." Several years later this man came to the school one morning, escorting his four daughters, intending to admit them. The principal was shocked. "You've been attacking us all this time," she exclaimed. "Why do you, of all people, now want to bring your daughters here?" He replied, "In this day and age, my daughters will not be able to get married if I cannot give them a dowry. I cannot afford a dowry. So my wife told me that if they are educated they can earn their own dowries and will be seen as an asset." Economic and social incentives are important drivers in spurring change even among those who are most resistant to change.

Within another half generation there will be massive change in many of these countries with respect to women's participation in society. This will happen because of two major factors that parallel what happened in American society and that contributed to women's empowerment here. First, as women get more highly educated, they will be enabled to work on par with men in an increasingly knowledge-based economy. Second, as societies prosper and women inherit, earn, and own greater wealth, they will use their wealth to improve women's rights. As Americans, we do not face as many cultural prohibitions on women's rights (there are still some), but we can help Muslim women gain the tools they need to make that leap in achieving equality.

The WISE Project is also making some progress on the very distressing issue of female genital cutting, or FGC—what used to be called, incorrectly, female circumcision. Among Muslims, however, and in many of the African countries where FGC is practiced, uneducated people believe that it is required by the Quran—which it absolutely is not.

The WISE Shura Council has issued a very strong opinion, argued entirely within the traditions of Islamic jurisprudence, against FGC. It is rare that a case is so obvious in Islamic law; I think of it as a slam-dunk. The challenge, however, one that is being taken up wonderfully by WISE, is to provide sermons and legal opinions to Islamic leaders and to help women understand that they do not need to inflict this harmful practice on their daughters to satisfy their religion; in fact, quite the contrary. The WISE Project has partnered with an Egyptian NGO, the Egyptian Association for Society and Development (EASD), to provide appropriate religious education as well as economic incentives to deter those currently performing FGC.

In 2008, for example, the EASD persuaded a barber who had an illegal side business in FGC that the practice was un-Islamic and harmful to women. In exchange for new barber's tools and some monetary compensation, he not only stopped the practice; he proudly displays to all his customers (in his thriving shop) a declaration from al-Azhar University that FGC is *haraam*. In another case, a poor widowed Egyptian midwife agreed to stop practicing FGC in exchange for an investment in her start-up grocery and poultry store.

I know that to many non-Muslim Americans, a marriage between Islam and feminism seems bizarre, but that perception is based on taking traditional cultural practices in Muslim-majority countries for Islamic practice itself. It also comes from not knowing the context in which major changes occur in the Muslim world (such as women becoming *muftiyyah*s, which does not make headlines in the United States). In fact there is a natural partnership between Muslim women activists and feminist movements in the United States, secular as well as religious, and around the world.

Our initiatives such as the WISE Project are having a powerful catalytic effect on the ground, putting the principles of a moderate, egalitarian, justice-seeking, merciful, and compassionate Islam into concrete practice. We help create openings, doors through what had been considered walls. Once we open one of these doors a little bit, others open them wider, allowing and encouraging thousands of women to pour through. We help men and women create social change in the context of their faith, change that inspires genuine social transformation.

Dress, Worship, and Culture

Since there has been so much controversy about women's dress in Muslim countries and in the West, and so much verbiage about what "true Islam" requires, it is probably best to begin a discussion on the topic by differentiating between a society's dress codes and what God requires of us. There are Muslims in many different countries, and most so-called Muslim practices are in fact the cultural practices of their societies.

Consider the question of worship and appropriate dress, especially head coverings. St. Paul weighed in early (1 Corinthians 11: 4–5): "Any man who prays or prophesies with something on his head disgraces his head, but any woman who prays or prophesies with her head unveiled disgraces her head—it is one and the same thing as having her head shaved." There are relatively few contemporary Christians who would make the argument as strenuously as St. Paul, but traditionally in the United States Christian women have worn hats or scarves in church and men automatically took their hats off. The practices have become cultural norms far more than religious edicts.

Among Jews, the skullcap, known as the *yarmulke* (in Yiddish) or *kippah* (in Hebrew), has a conflicted history for both men and women. The Talmud argues for it (for men), but there is no apparent biblical injunction to wear one. Jewish denominations and movements have differed over a head covering during worship for over a century. While it has become far more common for Conservative and Reform Jewish women to wear *kippot* during services, there are still many Reform men and women who choose not to. Only the most religiously conservative Jews would argue that God ignores the prayers of those with a different head covering.

Similarly how Muslims dress when they pray is generally shaped by culture and tradition more than by legal precept. In Malaysia, for example, women commonly wear hijabs (headscarves) and clothes with brightly colored patterns, revealing only their face and hands. This dress satisfies the most conservative religious ruling on what must be covered for the prayers to be valid. Whenever they do their daily prayers, however, whether at home or at the mosque, most Malaysian women put on a two-piece white head covering and a white tunic called a *telukong,* often over their colorful clothes and their hijab. For most of them it is psychologically difficult, almost impossible, to pray without wearing this outfit. And the *telukong,* of course, receives no mention in the Quran or the *Hadith.*

That said, scholars debated the question of what men and women need to wear during prayer (for the prayer to be valid) centuries ago. All schools of law hold that if men are covered from the navel to the knee their prayers are valid, but I have yet to see a man praying in a mosque shirtless. All this goes to show that cultural influences are often more determinative than religious requirements.

For women, the cultural and legal issues have been a little more complicated. In the Prophet's time social class dictated whether or not a woman had to cover her head. Because slave women frequently went bareheaded, scholars held that they could pray bareheaded as well. On the other hand, the fact that it was culturally common for most women to cover their heads in the desert climate of Arabia in the Prophet's time led to the practice of most women covering their head in prayer. A cultural norm in effect solidified into a religious norm, even though some scholars held different opinions on whether it was legally necessary.

Although covering one's head during prayer is rarely controversial, the issue of covering in public has become so; in fact the issue has intensified in the past three or four decades, for several reasons. First, in the years after their defeat in the 1973 war with Israel, in which hardly any family did not lose at least one relative, Egyptians flocked to mosques and became far more religiously observant—and Egypt is the most populous country in the Arab world. Then in the mid-1970s, when oil prices climbed dramatically, Saudi Arabia became a much wealthier country and imported many thousands of relatively uneducated workers from Muslim-majority nations such as Egypt, Pakistan, Bangladesh, Nigeria, and Indonesia. Many of these workers believed that Saudi Arabian Islam, being the Islam of the Holy Land, was unchanged since the Prophet's time, and so whatever the religious and clothing norms of Saudi Arabia were, these began to be imported into major Muslim population centers. Likewise Jewish friends tell me that the experience of going to Israel, where Orthodox Judaism dominates the religious landscape, sometimes persuades young Conservative or Reform Jews that Orthodoxy or Ultra-Orthodoxy is the only "legitimate" Judaism. Such is the power of a Holy Land's cultural practices over the faith of many millions.

The intensification of religious nationalism and extremism in many Muslim countries has further reinforced the most conservative cultural norms, putatively under the guise of following Islamic law. So instead of demonstrating respect for different interpretations of Islamic law, since the mid-1970s increasing numbers of Muslims have been acting more conservatively both in their religious practice and in their cultural norms and are expressing much less tolerance for authentic and legitimate differing interpretations of Islamic law and practice.

The issue of women's dress and head coverings has become a painful issue not only in Europe, but in America as well, as more hard-line men and some women are pressuring all women to cover their heads and criticize or attack women who refuse as "not Muslim enough." One young Muslim woman told me that, at the Islamic Society of North America conference in 2010, a man she did not know declared that she would go to hell for not wearing the hijab.

What is most important for American Muslims is to encourage our fellow believers to be godly, to pay attention to the Second Commandment, and to really care about others as ourselves—rather than to bash them on the head with a hijab, literally or figuratively, and with our own religious dogma. In our mosques today worshippers need to focus on their inner state of real connection to God and worry less about imposing cultural dress norms on others when we leave the mosque. We need to be *encouraging* people to join us in prayer, not drawing sartorial lines in the sand that drive others away from worshipping God. If we focus on really getting and staying connected to the spiritual and ethical principles of our faith, and worry less about these externalities, we and our religion will be so much better off. In America, with the tremendous cultural range of believers and practicing Muslims, it is particularly obvious that we need to respect the differences of others.

Given all of the political and media attention to Muslim women's dress, it is all the more important to understand the history of the issue and the way cultural contexts have evolved over time. All societies, after all, have dress codes, even if they are not written down. Plumbers dress differently from police; college students dress differently from nurses. Context matters too: we dress differently for a picnic than for a wedding or a funeral. In Arabian society at the time of the Prophet, culturally determined dress codes for distinct social groups—principally Bedouins, townsfolk, and slaves—gave practical form to injunctions regarding the parts of the body to be shielded from public gaze, known as the *awra,* under Islamic law.

The key, in the Quran, is that God urges modesty in dress in terms of physical exposure, personal adornment, and behavior with respect to the opposite sex. (The rabbis of the Talmud often stressed the virtue of modesty in attire as well.) The critical passage is this: "Say to the believing men that they should lower their gaze and guard their private parts: that will make for greater purity for them: and God is well acquainted with all that they do. And say to the believing women that they should lower their gaze and guard their private parts; and not to display their adornments" (Quran 24:30–31). In the same passage God says that women should cover their "pocket," interpreted as their cleavage, because women traditionally "pocketed" money and other small items in their cleavage, which prosperous Meccan women, like their Western eighteenth- and nineteenth-century counterparts, used to accentuate. God also tells women not to flaunt their "adornments," including a specific injunction not to stamp one's foot while wearing an otherwise hidden ankle bracelet, a seventh-century Arab form of flirtation.

The issue here is not the precise amount of bodily exposure, which varies from culture to culture, but, again, the question of context and intent. The Quran recommends against bold sexual approaches, sexually flirtatious interactions, or immodest exposure of the body in the context of Arab cultural norms at the time. In most Muslim cultures even today, whether in Asia, North Africa, or the Middle East, you will not see men and women being physically affectionate in public, even if they are married. Clearly this is a cultural issue rather than a religious one. After all, regardless of religious creed or national or cultural background, few married couples would engage in a long intimate kiss in a crowded public park (except, perhaps, in Paris). And in India, China, and Japan, few couples greet each other with kisses in public at all.

Consider dancing at a wedding or large social event. The stately waltz, today considered a very chaste dance in the United States, would be considered as flagrantly sexual in many countries as the belly dance is here. Muslim women do a traditional folk dance together in mixed company at weddings in Kashmir, something they would do only among themselves at a Saudi Arabian wedding. These differences have nothing to do with Islam, only with the governing culture.

From culture to culture and era to era, women cover and uncover different parts of their bodies for many different reasons, ranging from what they understand to be a religious requirement to an interest in asserting their identity at different stages of their lives and whether they are interviewing for a job or playing soccer. In Iran during the days of the shah, for instance, women wore the hijab to indicate their opposition to the regime; today, when women are forced to wear the hijab by the regime, they wear it loosely as a way of opposing the current regime.

Still Western standards of physical display and physical intimacy pose something of a challenge for most Muslims. In African American communities, Black Muslim women who wore the hijab were considered sexually off limits. As a teenager in New York, I remember hearing young men who normally delighted in flirtatious street banter warning, "Don't mess with them Muslims." Women felt protected from sexual scrutiny by their scarves—as they did at the time of the Prophet.

There are several reasons women give for wearing the hijab in the West. First, and most obviously, it is an act of piety. Second, they wish to assert or declare their religious identity publicly—a powerful statement when they feel that this identity is under attack. Third, the hijab may emphasize that they wish to be defined less by their looks than by their brains. Some women feel physically safer around men when they are covered.

In my friend James Zogby's book *Arab Voices,* he quoted a conversation he had on a plane with a young Saudi Arabian woman attending college in the United States who was on her way home. As she put on her traditional robe before landing, Zogby asked if "she minded covering—especially the *niqab,* or face veil. 'No,' she said without hesitation, 'in fact I miss it. In the States I get tired of being leered at. Covered, I'm in control. I can walk where I please and engage only when it suits me, and I can be seen only by those whom I want to see me.'"

But many American women argue, quite reasonably, that they should not have to modify their dress to avoid boorish behavior; they should be free to dress however they wish and not have to worry about harassment. This is an immensely complicated issue about which people feel passionately on all sides. Some who argue that the only question is what a woman wishes to wear draw the line when women in America choose to wear the hijab or the niqab. Perhaps they don't trust that such a woman is making a completely free choice. But what do they think about Orthodox Jewish women's traditional attire, or that of Amish women?

These examples highlight how few of us make entirely individually determined choices regarding fashion. Each of our cultures has norms, and when different cultures bump up against each other, so do their norms. The fact that fashion has to do with sexuality means that the interaction of different cultural norms can be volatile.

American culture itself puts enormous pressure on all of us. It has become dramatically more sexually explicit in the past decade, and appears to be accelerating in this direction, spurred on, I think, by the Internet. We have to put filters on our home computers so our children do not stumble onto pornographic websites; everyday speech, including on television and radio, uses words unthinkable just ten years ago; and the hypersexualization of women's clothing is now invading prepubescent girls' fashions. Magazines explicitly link display of cleavage to female self-esteem. Young women and young men routinely display their underwear outside tank tops and jeans as a matter of fashion.

How are we Muslims to reconcile Quranic recommendations of modesty with this culture? For one thing, we don't have to. Muslim women by and large have rejected what they see as the oversexualization of American fashion. They have chosen modesty. That does not mean, however, that they are importing the cultural mores and sartorial standards of Arabian society in the seventh or seventeenth century into twenty-first-century America. No one in a Muslim community in New York should pressure Muslim girls to wear the niqab or the burka. On the contrary, in a trend that I expect to continue and develop, savvy entrepreneurs are developing new lines of fashionable clothing for Muslim women, including hijabs.

And who knows? Perhaps the growing number of American Muslim women will be responsible for helping to swing the pendulum of young women's fashions in a different direction. Many non-Muslims, I suspect, would be thrilled with such a change. In any event, women themselves will take the lead in these matters. Like most young women, young American Muslim women can be exceptionally inventive in matters of fashion. They know how to mix and match, so to speak, to draw from popular American culture and the fashions of their mothers' and grandmothers' cultures to create new ways of dressing.

For more than a century daughters of native-born Americans, and especially immigrants, have been pushing against their mothers' and fathers' traditional cultural norms and limits and redrawing the boundaries of acceptable behavior. Russians and Italians, West Indians and Pakistanis, Latinas and Asians, all immigrated from cultures—Jewish, Protestant, Catholic, Muslim, Buddhist, Hindu, Confucian—in which girls were expected to obey patriarchal authority in the family and play roles subservient to men, especially in public. Girls and young women gained more freedom and autonomy in America the longer they lived here. That freedom and autonomy has included matters of dress as well as schooling, social life, employment, gender roles, musical preferences, choice of a spouse, timing of marriage, religious practice, and family size.

Muslim girls and young women are part of this movement, in America and around the world, whether or not they realize it. My guess is that their parents understand it more deeply, if not always happily. The critical task will be to help them sort out what is essential and timeless in their religion, and what is mainly a matter of cultural context. Those of us charged with religious leadership have special responsibilities to help our people make these distinctions and to avoid the temptation to judge our children and those with whom we disagree.

My role as an imam is to help people evolve in their spirituality and be the very best Muslims they can be. Muslims in America have to learn how to become part of what, at its best, is a deeply tolerant and nonjudgmental people. That is as much the American as it is the Islamic ethos. I will not pretend that this tolerance cannot get us in trouble with Muslims in more culturally conservative countries. But in many *hadiths* the Prophet warned his followers against judging others. In one, he said, "A man may do what seems to the people righteous, but he can be one of the dwellers in hell. Another may do what seems to be the work of a dweller of hell, but actually be a resident of Paradise" (Bukhari 6238). Therefore, I firmly believe, and have no problem arguing on Quranic grounds, that it is in line with American and Muslim values to be as nonjudgmental as possible, to leave judgment where it belongs: with God.

Marriage and Identity

As an imam practicing in New York City for almost thirty years who has traveled the United States and the world, I believe it is critical for

American Muslims and religious scholars to address the real issues that exist in our societies and our communities, and not hide our heads in the sand. If we do not undertake these discussions, our fellow Muslims will feel that their religion has nothing to say to them about some of the most intimate and pressing realities of their lives.

It is our responsibility to provide pastoral care to our people, to understand their lives and the pressures on them and their families and communities. It is my responsibility to take what I know of the Quran and Islamic law and make that wisdom available to my community and relevant to their practical as well as spiritual lives.

All nations, groups, and communities, whether they are ethnic, cultural, or religious, seek to preserve their group identity. Here is a dilemma, one that has been faced by nearly all religions at one point or another, especially during a major historical transition, such as immigration, exile, or globalization. I am talking about interfaith marriage, particularly the question of whether a Muslim woman can marry a non-Muslim man, but also marriages within the faith between different cultures. Why are these so fraught? Because, for religious as well as sociological reasons, interfaith (and intercultural) marriages are where cultural assimilation and integration enter a nitty-gritty reality.

As American Jews and Catholics have learned, mothers tend to have far more influence than fathers over the religious education of their children. So when men marry out of the faith, parents and grandparents worry—with reason—that the children will be raised in the wife's religion, and there will be fewer Jews or Catholics in the world. Religious authorities in America have always worried out loud about assimilation, and this type of assimilation is the most erosive of cultural identity.

This issue is a little different in the Muslim community. Under classical Islamic law, Muslim men are allowed to marry believing women among the People of the Book—traditionally Jews or Christians—without requiring their bride to convert to Islam. As a result, many Muslim men marry non-Muslims, thus reducing the supply of Muslim men for Muslim women.

On the other hand, also under classical Islamic law, the general opinion is that a Muslim woman may not marry a non-Muslim man unless he converts to Islam. Why are Muslim women not allowed to marry People of the Book?

A group of foreign imams visited our office under the U.S. State Department's Foreign Visitors Program in 2011. They were keen to know how we handled this issue because, they informed us, this very dilemma was becoming acute in their nations. All over the Muslim world today, including the Gulf countries, increasing numbers of young professionals from the West and other nations go to work, meet a local Muslim woman, and fall in love and want to get married. What are the imams to do? Even in the traditional Muslim homelands, religious leaders are now being forced to substantively address this vital social issue.

The Prophet said in a *hadith* that he regarded marriage as equal to fulfilling half of one's religion (Bayhaqi 5486). That is how much he encouraged marriage. God's directive in the Quran, through the teachings of the Prophet and the understanding of centuries of jurisprudence, is crystal clear: men *and* women ought to be married. Since it is so much easier for Muslim men to marry outside of the faith, are Muslim women to be left unmarried? Since denying women opportunities for marriage is not a good thing, should not women then be given the same permission as men?

Here is what I think, and what is now guiding my own practice. In the Quran (5:5) God expressly allows believing men (Muslims) to marry women of the People of the Book, but He is silent on whether believing women can marry men of the People of the Book. By probing the reasons that allow Muslim men to marry People of the Book, we may be able to determine the conditions that may allow Muslim women to marry Jewish and Christian men. But there ought to be certain provisos, given the very real historical difference in women's attention to children's religious education, as well as their own.

First, the non-Muslim husband-to-be has to agree that the woman can practice her religion freely, including being able to pray, keep the fast of Ramadan (which Muslims observe by getting up before dawn and having a light meal), go on the *hajj* if possible at least once, and not be forced to drink alcohol or consume pork in the home. Also, if she chooses to raise her children as Muslim, she should be able to do so. And he needs to be willing to put all this in writing.

Second, he has to believe in God and to believe that Muhammad was *a* prophet of God, even if not necessarily *the* prophet he follows. (Muslims believe as a matter of faith in Moses and Jesus as prophets and therefore deeply respect them, so this is about reciprocity.) He should not have to follow the Prophet's religious practice; he is not converting to Islam, after all. Most men are comfortable reciting the *shahada*—"I bear witness that there is no god but God and I bear witness that Muhammad is God's Messenger"—with this understanding, and it *so* pleases the bride's parents. And it should not be so difficult for him; Muhammad was, after all, a genuine historical figure. Here is the reasoning: if he neither believes in God nor that Muhammad was a prophet, how can she be expected to speak freely with him about her religion?

If the couple are aligned in this way, I see no Islamic legal objection to such a wedding; in fact I feel quite positively about Islamic law supporting it. I know that people often consider those of us in the religion business as impractical dreamers, a little like college professors with a spiritual bent. In reality we deal with people's lives in the most concrete ways: how they love, worship, marry, have children, divorce, and face death.

If I can conduct a "mixed" wedding, help both parties understand their religious lives and commitments, keep at least one within the faith, help them see their marriage as a sacred bond, and help keep them part of a loving community, the Muslim community can support them and help bring more joy, love, and Godly commitment into the world. Alternatively—and this happens all the time—narrow-minded religious leaders can tell them their love is breaking the rules, and give them the message that the Muslim community can do nothing for them religiously.

How do you think people in love, particularly young people, respond to such scolding? They flee, religiously, psychologically, and even physically, seeking out a justice of the peace for a civil ceremony that may break their parents' hearts. For years they may tell the story of the rigid imam who, instead of trying to keep them connected to the faith, casually dismissed them as religious rule breakers.

Why would we do such a thing? Aside from its needless emotional cruelty, it will not build our community, neither our faith community nor our sense of and commitment to a larger multifaith community. And if in theological terms we embrace Judaism and Christianity through prophets and scriptures, why not in our homes as well? What could be wrong with a child learning the best of Judaism, Christianity, and Islam?

The choice I have made, and now promote, is to accept these couples, help them, and hope that they will help sustain and build our community. Immigration, migration, exile, and globalization are real and massive global movements, but they all play out in the economic, emotional, and spiritual lives of people who come for advice to religious leaders.

There is even an instructive precedent of some importance on this subject from the Prophet's own life. The Prophet's eldest daughter from his marriage to Khadijah, Zainab, had married her cousin before Muhammad became the Prophet. When her father did become the Prophet, she accepted Islam, but her husband did not. In spite of pressures from his family to divorce Zainab, they stayed married, as he deeply loved Zainab, Khadijah (his aunt), and the Prophet. After the Prophet fled Mecca for Medina, the Meccans waged war against him, and in the first battle against the Prophet, Zainab's husband was drafted and fought on the side of the Meccans. The Meccans lost and Zainab's husband was taken captive. The Prophet offered to free the

Meccan prisoners for a ransom. When the ransom for the husband's release arrived, the Prophet recognized the onyx necklace Zainab had sent. It had belonged to Khadijah, who had given it to her daughter as a wedding gift. The Prophet was overcome with the memory of his late wife, returned the necklace to his daughter, and released her husband—who later embraced Islam.

Look carefully at this story. When the Prophet's own daughter was married to a man who did not accept Islam, he did not force her to break off the marriage. Even after her husband had taken up arms against Islam, against his own father-in-law, the Prophet refused to accept his daughter's ransom and instead released his son-in-law. Instead of denying his daughter or her husband, he engaged the two of them in such a way that his former enemy was transformed. From that story we learn that our true task in life is to engage others in a positively transformative manner, rather than deny their reality or personhood. This is precisely what Martin Luther King Jr. meant by the transforming power of God's love.

The power of God's love, in addition to helping us be the faithful believers we are all called to be, can empower Muslim women, both in America and around the world. As presidents, heads of households, and founders of NGOs, women are active agents of social change. And as they continue to transform the world, we must also remember that this revolutionary feminism is centrally rooted in Islamic tradition.

We live in a society undergoing transformations and revolutions, and American Muslim religious leaders must look to our own historical precedents to figure out real-world solutions to difficult problems rather than put blinders on and say "No, please leave my office—what you are doing is *haraam*." The Prophet is our guide.

5

OUR FIGHT AGAINST EXTREMISM

Terror in Washington, D.C.

It was March 9, 1977, about 3:30 in the afternoon. I was in my office at Process Equipment & Supply Company, a filtration equipment company in Union City, New Jersey, and the phone rang. It was my sister in Washington, D.C. "Dad and Mom are being held hostage," she shouted, "along with some other employees. Turn on the radio!" I did what she said. There was a hostage crisis in Washington; someone had been shot; gunmen were holding people in three locations, including the Islamic Center on Embassy Row.

I was twenty-eight years old and had just started work as a sales engineer. What on earth was going on? What could my parents have done to deserve this?

My mind was racing. Why? How? Who? I kept thinking back to 1965, when we first arrived in the United States from Egypt. My father directed the Islamic Center of New York City and then, five years later, the Center in D.C. You know how, even after a lit match goes out, you can still smell the sulfur that burned when the match first flared up? Well, the smell of sulfur was still in the New York air when we arrived.

Malcolm X had been assassinated just a few months earlier. He had broken with Elijah Muhammad's Nation of Islam—which most Americans knew as the Black Muslims—and become what we call an orthodox Muslim, like other Muslims around the world. Malcolm had spent a lot of time with my father's predecessor, who had convinced him to go on the *hajj,* which he wrote about so movingly in his autobiography. During the *hajj* Malcolm witnessed individuals of all races worshipping equally and together, which inspired him to join the mainstream Muslim community. Unlike Elijah Muhammad's Nation of Islam, mainstream Islam has never made distinctions between human beings on the basis of race.

The intensity and rawness of the emotions around race, Islam, religion, and politics in 1960s America was very different from what I'd seen growing up in Malaysia and Egypt. I became aware of the bubbling emotions that existed in the collective unconscious of African Americans at the time, their frustration around the heritage of slavery, the competition within various factions of the African American community, including between Muslims and Christians. This was the first time in my life I witnessed Islam associated with any form of racism and violence.

But the 1960s were behind us, I thought on that terrible March day. How could my parents be held hostage? My father had already been in Washington for seven years. What had happened? Thankfully, a colleague offered to drive me to Newark Airport. I was a mess, and my mind was in chaos, but I took the next shuttle flight to Washington within an hour. With all the arrogance and hubris of youth, my plan was to personally negotiate my parents' release. Of course that was ridiculous: I was much too involved and had no experience negotiating anything.

The most shocking thing to me in that situation was that *it was Muslims* who had taken my parents hostage. We later discovered that they were members of a sect (named after a school of Islamic law, the Hanafi), founded in 1958 by the former national secretary of the Nation of Islam in New York, an apparently unstable fellow named

Hamaas Abdul Khaalis, who published an open letter critical of the Nation and Elijah Muhammad in 1972. He had arrived at his house one day in 1973 to find five of his children, his baby grandson, and another man shot to death. Khaalis blamed Elijah Muhammad (whom many suspected of ordering Malcolm X's death), and although the killers were caught and sentenced to life in prison, he was angry that Elijah went free.

Early that afternoon Khaalis and two accomplices burst into the Islamic Center of Washington, D.C., where he held my father and mother and nine other staff members and visitors hostage. For thirty-nine excruciating hours he pointed a rifle at my father—who had never had a gun pointed at him before—and for much of that time the trigger was cocked. "You attack us," Khaalis told the hostages, and later the police, "and Rauf will be the first to die." My mother would also have been killed.

All the ambassadors of the Muslim-majority countries—Iran, Pakistan, Egypt, Saudi Arabia, Indonesia, and Malaysia—were on the board of the Center, and they adored my father. I remember the Iranian ambassador—a wealthy man, a playboy about town, who loved my father—saying to the police, "What do they want? If it's money, I'll pay the ransom." The police rejected recourse to a ransom, but he, along with the ambassadors from Egypt and Pakistan, worked around the clock negotiating with Khaalis, reading him Quranic passages, eventually even going to meet with him at the Islamic Center, helping to work out a deal.

What seemed to have made the most difference in negotiating with Khaalis, according to the Pakistani ambassador, was this passage from the Quran (5:2): "And let not the hatred of some people in shutting you out of the Sacred Mosque lead you into transgression and hostility on your part; help one another in righteousness and piety, but judge not one another in sin and rancor." The reconciling, nonjudgmental power of the passage had a real effect on Khaalis, who surely felt shut out of America and of the community of American Muslims.

What a powerful verse! It is our responsibility as believers to help those who hate us discover the best parts of themselves—righteousness and piety—and not the worst: sin and rancor. This verse also points to the vicious circle that extremism produces: if we react to sin and rancor, we create an endless self-sustaining tribal blood feud that can set people and nations against each other for centuries, long after the original injury has been forgotten.

After nearly two days my parents were released. We were relieved, of course, but intense introspection regarding the event inevitably ensued. What was this all about? What was going on in our community? Why were Muslims doing such things to each other? Even though Khaalis had previously been judged mentally ill in an unrelated case, and this was an isolated incident, we knew that American Muslims needed to step up to the plate of religious tolerance and bridge building—without a rifle and cocked trigger pointing at us.

When people recall the 1977 hostage crisis in Washington, they never remember my parents' involvement. What they remember is that gunmen took B'nai B'rith headquarters hostage, abusing the people who were there and ranting about the Jews controlling the courts; that the "Hanafis" shot and killed a young black radio reporter and a policeman, and wounded City Councilman Marion Barry. The long *Time* magazine article on the siege and its resolution did not even mention my parents' names—though to be fair, it gave enormous credit to the three Muslim ambassadors who negotiated an end to the siege. Still, Muslim victims of Muslim violence apparently did not rise to the level of historical significance.

There is a strong feeling among Muslims in the United States and abroad that to Westerners, we count less. The same pundits who denounce Islamist terrorists pay little attention to the fact that Muslims have been the most numerous victims of worldwide terrorism since the 9/11 attacks on the United States. In 2009, according to the U.S. State Department, some 58,000 people were killed or injured in terrorist attacks, at least half of whom were Muslims, in Iraq, Afghanistan, Pakistan, Congo, Somalia, Russia, and South Asia.

Here are the questions we Muslims ask. How many Americans could come close to identifying the correct proportion of Muslims among the total? Which news outlets featured the proportion of Muslim victims? Why are the stories of Muslim victims told so rarely? The entire world reads the American press, so what kind of impact does it have on the Muslim world to know that Muslim victims of terrorism are routinely ignored? And finally, think of how it might affect Americans' views of Islam and Muslims to know how much Muslims suffer from extremist violence.

The Vicious Circle of Extremist Ideology

Extremists of all religions excite the worst, most extreme reactions from others. Extremist religion provides a channel for disaffected nihilists and unstable people to express their alienation and violent fantasies; after all, in a population of 1.6 billion, there will be some genuinely crazy and dangerous people. Back in 1993, when I read Samuel Huntington's article "The Clash of Civilizations" in *Foreign Affairs,* in which he identified Islam as the next existential enemy of Western civilization, I thought, "By effectively declaring ideological war on the Muslim world, you will create and precipitate the very reality that you fear so much."

Attitudes create reality. When Muslims read presumably respectable manifestos predicting a bloody battle between Western and Islamic civilizations, some will want to act accordingly, and preemptively. The book that came out of Huntington's article became a bestseller in the West *and* in Muslim-majority countries, where it was very influential—and amplified Muslims' perception that we were now America's next enemy. Scholars, policymakers, and public officials throughout these countries discussed the book very seriously. Were the American guns that had been aimed at the Soviet Union in Afghanistan, some in Muslim hands, now going to be turned toward them? How could

Huntington not have realized that some of those same guns would now be aimed in self-defense at the United States?

Words matter everywhere, especially as part of a developed ideology or worldview. Extremist ideology leads to extremist actions. It takes only one dramatic extremist action to polarize moderate people and light the fuse of conflict, which sets off tit-for-tat explosions in a vicious, violent, and snowballing cycle of action and reaction. And if there is a ready-made ideology waiting for the newly polarized, it accelerates the conversion process.

Osama bin Laden, who fought originally on the side of the United States against the Soviet Union, was influenced by the well-known Egyptian extremist thinker Sayyid Qutb, who claimed that the entire West was composed of infidels and that Muslim leaders throughout the world were colluding with the West against Islam—which in his interpretation made it acceptable to fight and kill them. Qutb was the most influential theorist and ideologue of twentieth-century Muslim extremism, and he found a follower in Ayman al-Zawahiri, bin Laden's second in command, and then in bin Laden himself. Huntington's work appeared to prove America's true colors toward Muslims in the minds of bin Laden and many others.

In the United States we have no shortage of anti-Islamic ideologues, but probably none as respectable and influential as Huntington, who persuaded many Washington policymakers (and would-be policymakers), pundits, think-tank personnel, and journalists to think of some monolith called Islam as their—and the West's—enemy. Huntington was the Qutb of the West, making famous such inflammatory statements as "Islam has bloody borders." (And Christianity does not?)

As the building blocks of extremist worldviews, ideas matter. Qutb's worldview helped convince many in the Muslim world that America invaded Iraq and Afghanistan to eradicate Islam, even though the United States had been the major funder of the mujahedeen in Afghanistan. Such apparently plausible analyses as Huntington's (which continues to be quoted approvingly today) created an enemy before anyone had even heard of Osama bin Laden.

The task and challenge now, for Muslims and non-Muslims alike, is to reverse that self-reinforcing dynamic and instead promote a worldview true to genuine Muslim values that returns kindness and generosity for hatred and is not suckered into a battle of simplistic, inaccurate, extremist, profoundly dangerous worldviews. After the right-wing Norwegian Anders Breivik killed seventy-seven people, mostly teenagers, in a terrorist attack in July 2011, it became clear that the views of extremist American Islamophobes had helped nourish his murderous ideology. Extremist worldviews can have very serious consequences indeed.

That is why I found General Colin Powell's extraordinary statement on *Meet the Press* on October 19, 2008, so moving. In response to attempts to slur presidential candidate Barack Obama as a Muslim, Powell was offering a counternarrative, one that, taken seriously, could reverse the hate-and-response dynamic:

> But the really right answer is, "What if he is? Is there something wrong with being a Muslim in this country?" . . . Is there something wrong with some seven-year-old Muslim American kid believing that he or she could be President? Yet, I have heard senior members of my own Party [suggest] he's Muslim and he might be associated with terrorists. This is not the way we should be doing it in America. . . . Now, we have got to stop polarizing ourselves in this way.

In the Quran (6:108) God tells us not to insult the beliefs of others lest they take revenge by insulting God in their ignorance. In other words, humility in our understanding of God's purposes *requires* us to be respectful of other religions. I may not believe what you believe, but both you and I must be free to honestly, respectfully, and in a friendly way reject each other's beliefs, to say to each other, in the words of the Quran (109:6), "To you your religion, and to me my religion."

Religious Difference or Religious Conflict?

It therefore distresses me when adherents of any faith act with disdain or violence or scorn toward other religions. When Muslims treat others this way, either other religious communities or Muslims holding differing opinions well within the realm of Islamic thought, such as the differences between Sunni and Shia, I find it infuriating because it so violates Quranic teachings. The Quran recognizes different languages and forms of worship as being authorized by prophets God sent to every community. How are we to know which messengers came to different peoples, and whether they might be following God's word? We do not have to worship as they do; God instructs us to acknowledge theological, doctrinal, and liturgical differences without hostility.

That is why we Muslims are required to protect all religious sites, even though we may disagree with their theology, even though they may not be monotheistic. Otherwise the principle that there shall be no compulsion in religion would be overturned. The Taliban destruction of the Buddhas of Bamiyan was not only an offense against Buddhism and the destruction of a world cultural treasure—it was also contrary to Islamic law, its presumed justification.

We Muslims must revive our practice of valuing and protecting all other faith traditions, especially those of Jews and Christians, as they are the closest to our religious and geographic heritage. To make my point about how nomenclature ossifies our thinking, I often ask Christians to consider Muslims as Unitarians with an Arabic liturgy. To which I get a roar of laughter. The point is that we are within the spectrum of Christian theology. After all, many of our theological differences with Christianity also existed *between* sects in Christianity's earliest centuries. Some medieval Christians even regarded Islam as a Christian heresy.

Those of us who believe in a single Creator need to spend more time focusing on what binds us together as communities of believers and create the basis for an overarching spiritual unity that can embrace our commonalities as well as our differences. We all need to understand other religions in terms of their theology, history, and narratives, and recognize how religious beliefs have contributed to conflict, yes, but also to decent and humane relations as well. When we focus on what divides us we tend to forget the genuine history of religious co-operation—between Muslims and Jews in particular.

Today perhaps the single most widespread myth about Muslims and Jews—among people of all faiths, in all countries, throughout the world—is that from the time of Ishmael and Isaac, Muslims and Jews have been existential enemies, blood enemies. The corollary, of course, is that this ancient history of enmity explains the modern conflict in the Middle East. But this is nonsense, a myth that can endure only by forgetting, suppressing, or rewriting Muslim and Jewish history. The truth is that the history of Muslims and Jews is far more intertwined, far more intimate, and more inspirational than most people in either group realize.

For example, and it is not a small example, most Muslims and Jews have forgotten the history described at the beginning of chapter 3, that it was the Muslim companion of the Prophet, Umar al-Khattab, the second caliph of Islam, who invited Jews to return to Jerusalem in the seventh century—after they had been expelled by Romans five centuries earlier. Think about this for a minute. There were conflicts, it's true, between the Prophet and a Jewish tribe in Medina, but if Muslims were blood enemies of the Jews why would Umar have invited Jewish families back into Jerusalem to live and worship freely?

Consider again that in the twelfth century, the Muslim leader Saladin (later sultan of Egypt) also invited Jews back to Jerusalem, after he had defeated the Crusaders, who had expelled them. And that Jews and Muslims lived peacefully under the Cordoba caliphate in Spain from the eighth to the eleventh centuries. When the great Jewish scholar Moses Maimonides went into exile from Spain—fleeing the oppression of a fundamentalist Muslim regime—he lived first in Morocco, and then spent the rest of his life in Egypt, where he was much honored and employed as the Muslim ruler's personal physician.

Most Jews know that the Catholic Inquisition evicted Jews from Spain in that momentous year 1492. Muslims know this date very well too, however, as the great majority of those evicted in 1492 were in fact Muslims. I confess that I do not know whether most Muslims or Jews know that the others joined them in forced conversion, exile, or conducting secret worship after public conversions to Christianity. Or that for centuries the Ottoman Empire ruled over Arabs and Turks, Armenians and Greeks, Christians, Orthodox, Jews, and Muslims, who all enjoyed substantial religious freedom. Or that during the terrible Holocaust of World War II Muslims in the Balkans and other regions saved thousands of Jews from the Nazis. Abdol Hossein Sardari, the Iranian ambassador in Paris during the war, saved more than 1,500 Jews by giving them Iranian passports.

With the cooperation of rabbis, imams, and laypeople around the country, American Muslims and American Jews are building the relationships that we know will demolish the myth of eternal enmity that has gained so much ground since the birth of Israel in 1948. These include Rabbis Marc Schneier, president of the Foundation for Ethnic Understanding; Ellen Lippman of Kolot Chaiyenu/Voices of Our Lives; Roland Matalon of B'nai Jeshurun; Joy Levitt of the Jewish Community Center in Manhattan; Robert Kaplan and Michael Miller of the Jewish Community Relations Council; Michael Paley of the United Jewish Congress; and Burton Visotzky from the Jewish Theological Seminary. Active Muslims include Dr. Ali Chaudry, president and cofounder of Center for Understanding Islam; Imam Yahya Hendi, Muslim chaplain at Georgetown University and the National Naval Medical Center; Imam Omar Abu Namous of the Islamic Center of New York; Dr. Ingrid Mattson, past president of the Islamic Society of North America (ISNA); Imam Muhammad Majid, the current ISNA president; Dr. Faroque Khan, past president of the Islamic Center of Long Island; and many others, particularly women in nonprofit organizations who are in many ways providing the infrastructure for substantial interfaith dialogue.

Nationalism and the Rise of Extremism

This multifaith coexistence has suffered greatly in the past century, especially in the past half-century. Religious nationalism became a more potent force after World War I and the dissolution of the Ottoman Empire. Since World War II ethnic and religious identity has become far more identified with nation-states. The marriage of religion and nationalism has nourished the rise of extremism across the Muslim world, whereby as one interpretation becomes politically or religiously "correct," others become politically incorrect or heretical. It then becomes an easy step to declare an action forbidden, *haraam*.

Too often now we see Muslim politicians, activists, and even religious leaders insisting that only one opinion is correct, and then enforcing it on an entire population, as the Taliban enforced the burka on the women of Afghanistan and Saudi Arabia recognizes only one "legitimate" school of law. Yet from the very beginning Muslim societies were far more pluralistic, far more open to diversity, and much more capable of embracing diversity for most of the past fourteen centuries—until as recently as fifty years ago. In the Quran (66:1, 5:87, 10:59) God explicitly criticizes believers, even the Prophet, for prohibiting that which God has permitted. We must bring back that openness to diversity.

Despite Quranic teaching, and in violation of Islamic religious ideals and history, after World War II a number of nationalist states insisted on becoming ethnic or religious monocultures. Yet when you make a pluralistic, multicultural nation monocultural, you impoverish it. Egyptian history provides a particularly painful example, one that is close to home for me. After the revolution in 1952, when Gamal

Abdel Nasser extolled Arab nationalism, Egyptian Jews who had been living in Egypt off and on since the time of the biblical Joseph, Greeks who had lived in Egypt since Alexander founded Alexandria (which remained a majority-Greek city until the mid-twentieth century), Italians who had lived in Egypt since the time of Julius Caesar and Cleopatra—all found their country less and less hospitable and decided to go into exile. Egypt lost their intellectual skills, business acumen, and financial capital. Egypt, which had been the undisputed leader of the Arab world, known to Arabs as *umm al-dunya,* "mother of the world," was impoverished materially, socially, politically, religiously, and culturally. The country lost its position of leadership in every area: literature, scholarship, film, the arts, and yes, even religion—another *Nakba* (calamity), in my opinion.

Juxtapose that catastrophe with the situation of the Gulf states now, prospering precisely because of the hard work and intellectual and cultural capital brought by foreign expatriates. Or, for that matter, consider the United States, the vibrant locus of so much diversity and creativity because it values the contributions of immigrants to its heritage, one we Muslims are enriching every day.

The creation of Pakistan as a separate Muslim state in the wake of Indian independence—the work of political activists, not religious scholars, who married a narrow version of Islam to nationalism—has led to decades of murderous conflict between India and Pakistan as each nation demonizes the other. Similarly the Zionist movement's success in founding Israel as a Jewish state was due to the efforts of political activists who successfully combined Jews' experience of religious persecution—from ancient times to the Holocaust—with nationalism. Even though, at its core, the Israeli-Palestinian conflict is a quarrel over land, each side's religious nationalism makes the dispute that much harder to resolve in rational terms. Nationalism, religion, and monoculturalism make for a dangerous cocktail. That is why we now need a multicultural, multifaith commitment to nonviolent solutions. A Jewish-Muslim, Arab-Jewish nonviolent movement could bring peace to the troubled Holy Land and usher in a new era of cooperation, prosperity, and happiness.

Analogously the Pakistan-India dispute is also over land, in this case over who will own Kashmir. And here too a Hindu-Muslim nonviolent movement will usher in peace and an era of cooperation and prosperity.

My hope is that eventually the current democratic ferment in the Arab world will bring about an era of relative democracy, religious tolerance, and good governance. Of course it is impossible to see the future clearly. Revolutions are messy, and when a revolution happens after decades of authoritarian rule, a chaotic, sometimes violent period ensues. But it is clear that in our modern era governments as well as their populations want to be part of the international family of nations. By rejecting the narrow monoculturalism of dictatorships under siege, they will help accelerate the interaction of people across cultures and religions.

More and more children are born today out of interethnic, interracial, and interfaith marriages, and the world is seeing a dramatic increase in people who identify with many different cultures. Our world may even be returning to ideas predating the nationalistic, monocultural nation-state. We Muslims, by getting in touch with the foundations of our faith, can help lead the way.

The Consequences of Religious Insult and Ignorance

Most Muslim antagonism toward Jews has nothing to do with religion and everything to do with land and nationalism: the question of Israel and the Palestinians. To the extent that Jews identify with Israel, that Israel continues and expands its occupation of Palestinian territory on religious grounds, and that many influential American Jews sustain a blanket endorsement of all Israeli government actions, there will be deep conflict between Muslims and Jews. Because this conflict—and not theological differences—has been *the* divisive issue between Jews and Muslims, I believe that when (not if) peace is made, Middle Eastern anti-Semitism will fade away.

That is why our interfaith work is important. Our rabbinical colleagues and counterparts, such as Rabbis David Saperstein, Michael Paley, and Irwin Kula of the National Jewish Center for Learning and Leadership, recognize the need to solve the Israel-Palestine conflict and are committed to working here in the United States toward exploring how we may contribute to such a desired end. As I have been arguing for decades, we Muslims have responsibilities in these matters as well. We need to disavow, and thereby undermine, the extremists among us. They accomplish the mirror image of what Islamophobes produce in the Muslim world: confirmation of their worst fears about the other.

Consider the Afghan reaction to the pathetically minor desecration of the Quran in March 2011 in Gainesville, Florida. As demonstrations swept Afghanistan in response, rioters attacked a UN compound, killing seven foreign workers. The Taliban issued statements condemning the desecration and supporting antiforeign rioters. But the fact that Pastor Terry Jones, a fanatical Christian extremist, engaged in true insults to our God and our faith was no excuse for violence against United Nations staff who had no connection to the mean-spirited pastor. God explicitly and repeatedly states in the Quran (6:164, 17:15, 35:18, 39:7; 53:38), "No soul bears the burdens [sins] of another." The Muslim extremists in Afghanistan violated this Quranic injunction by making an innocent soul bear the sin of another, which was not even a capital crime to begin with!

The use of force, ostensibly in the name of religion, to bring about justice has often resulted in force being used as a tool of false religion, of other agendas, usually political power, financial or material gain, or egotistic fame. This has resulted in the modern bane of the Muslim world: terrorism committed in God's name.

Many young disenchanted Muslim men are recruited into terrorist organizations because they see injustice and desire to establish justice. They are all too easily sucked into such movements by leaders motivated by political power, the desire for fame, or even material gain, who manipulate their faith and teach them to commit major sins like suicide bombing, which we have witnessed in the Muslim-majority countries of Afghanistan, Pakistan, Iraq, Indonesia, Egypt, Morocco, and, of course, Palestine. But justice is not established by fighting injustice with equal or greater injustice. The Prophet never condoned suicide under any circumstance, no matter what extremists claim about martyrs entering Paradise.

By taking the bait offered by the extremist pastor and other extremist Islamophobes, we Muslims embarrass ourselves and, in a striking example of circularity, end up reinforcing the very stereotypes held by those who hate us—all the while violating Shariah, God's law. To break this vicious circle we need instead to dig deeper into the origins and ethics of our faith and understand what we have in common with other genuine believers—particularly Christians and Jews—so that we cannot be thrown so easily by provocative acts thousands of miles away.

Muslim Nonviolence: How We Can Fight Extremism Successfully

How can we combat extremism in such a way that we do not create more extremists? How do we break this vicious circle? This was Martin Luther King Jr.'s problem as well, as he confronted an entrenched system of segregation maintained by millions of daily actions by tens of millions of Americans. His response was to build a multiracial, multifaith coalition of Protestants, Catholics, Jews, and secularists, all committed to fighting racism and segregation nonviolently. King's combination of this coalition and a nonviolent strategy had enough force to reverse the vicious cycle of racism and the extremism that it excited.

That is precisely what we need today: a nonviolent movement of

Muslims, Christians, Jews, Hindus, Buddhists, atheists, and others to come together and provide enough collective focused spiritual power to reverse the dynamics that are fueling extremism in both the Muslim and the Western world. We need such coalitions to attack an entire range of issues, including terrorism, women's rights, economic justice, and democracy. Spiritual power is primarily *nonviolent*; it is powerful, and it is transformative when focused. Among all the prophets this was especially Jesus' power.

In the words of the Quran, "Who speaks anything better than the one who calls [invites] people to God, does good, and says 'I am of those who submit?' [literally, I am of the Muslims]" (Quran 41:33). The word *islam* means "surrender"; its root, *salam,* means "peace." For starters, therefore, Muslims by their very name are required to surrender to God and taste the experience of being filled with the presence and remembrance of God. (Christians and Jews may hear an echo of Micah 6:8: "What does the Lord require of you but to do justice, and to love kindness, and to walk humbly with your God?")

The Quran (41:34–35) continues: "Good and evil are not equal. Repel evil with what is best until the one whom you have enmity with is transformed into a passionate friend. But none will attain that except those who persevere [or are patient], and none will attain that except those who are very lucky." There is an important *hadith* elaborating this point, in which the Prophet said, "The Muslim is someone who hurts no one, whether by his tongue or by his hand [by his words or his action]" (Nasa'i 4908).

These verses argue powerfully that the Quranic ethical ideal is nonviolence. God asserts in this verse the fundamental inequality and opposition of good and evil and recognizes the perennial battle between good and evil people and beings that He has put us to engage with. He commands us here not to repel evil with evil, not even evil with aggression, but to display the highest ethical standards that can transform the heart of the evil person.

This lesson is exhibited in the story of the first practitioner of nonviolence, Adam's son Abel, whose story is in both the Bible and the Quran. He and his brother Cain both made an offering to God, who accepted Abel's offering but rejected Cain's, presumably because something was wrong with the offering or with Cain's purity. This so aroused Cain's jealousy that he threatened to kill Abel. Even after the threat, Abel refused to respond in kind, saying, "Were you to raise your hand towards me to kill me, I won't ever raise my hand against you to kill you; for I fear God, the Lord of the worlds" (Quran 5:28).

What motivated Abel to absolute nonviolence was his "fear of God." The lesson here is that if we genuinely fear God, we must always do our utmost never to hurt another soul in any way at all, for we *will* be held accountable on Judgment Day for the hurt we commit—even an atom's weight worth of hurt (Quran 99:8).

The Prophet is described as compassionate and easily grieved by people's distress (Quran 9:128). Since we are urged to follow the Prophet's *sunna,* we too must be grieved by others' distress. That is as sure a sign of faith as delighting in others' distress is a sign of imperfection of faith. When we are filled with the Godly presence, our inner urge is to serve God, which is done both by performing acts of worship (First Commandment actions) and serving humanity (Second Commandment actions).

Prophets came to transform people into being the best they could be, in terms of both worshipping God and serving their fellow human beings. And like Jesus, the Prophet Muhammad brought the revelation that God condemns aggression, wants us not to be violent, and always urges us to forgiveness so that He will forgive us our sins and trespasses (Quran 24:22). It is time for Muslims to take the path of nonviolent struggle on behalf of peace and justice in ourselves and in our world.

When I shared with the prime minister of Malaysia my view that the key divide in the world was not between America—or the West—and the Muslim world but between all moderates of all regions and religions against the extremists of all regions and religions, he championed this idea into an effort to establish a "global movement of the moderates." He launched this idea in his UN General Assembly speech in October 2010 and developed his thoughts further in a brilliant speech delivered at Oxford University in May the following year. Both speeches drew strong positive responses from the White House, the U.S. State Department, and major European governments. He made the "global movement of the moderates" a commitment of the ASEAN nations at their summit meeting in Jakarta, Indonesia, on May 8, 2011, and on June 10 he held an international conference on the Quranic concept of *wasatiyyah* (moderation in faith) in Malaysia, from which base he has continued to champion the cause of rallying moderate Muslims and non-Muslims. In November 2011 he announced that Global Movement of the Moderates Foundation would be launched in January 2012.

This initiative draws powerful religious sustenance from a verse in which God says to the followers of the Prophet, "We have made you an *ummatan wasatan* [a moderate people, or a people of the Golden Mean] so that you can be a witness over people and the Prophet a witness over you" (Quran 2:143). Two important ideas are emphasized here: the importance of moderation and the idea of being a witness. In Arabic the word for "moderation" is much more powerful than in English, which suggests compromise, a weak balancing between two strong positions. In Arabic and in Islam "moderation" is an entire way of being and believing that is endorsed, encouraged, and emphasized by God's Messenger, the Prophet Muhammad, that encapsulates the principles of nonviolence. In many of his teachings, the Prophet emphasized that there was a limit to religiosity. He warned Muslims, "Avoid extremism [*al-ghuluw fi-ddin*], for people before you were led to destruction because of their extremism in religion" (ibn Hanbal 3655). This defines Islamic nonviolence, for extremist religiosity is violent religiosity, whereas perfection of faith, the opposite of extremism in religion, is, as exhibited by Abel, nonviolence.

The second important idea here is that of being a witness. The primary expression of faith is called by Muslims "the two *shahadas*," bearing witness to the oneness of God and bearing witness to Muhammad as Prophet. The notion of witness means fundamentally that we humans are accountable to and will be held accountable by God. But there is a reciprocal witnessing going on. God also witnesses and records all our actions, and on Judgment Day even our limbs will bear witness to what we have done in this life. But as in any court, to be a credible and qualified witness you have to have the right attributes: of speaking truthfully and not inventing falsehoods. Extremists are not credible witnesses. Even their testimony of faith is suspect! The verse also implies that moderation is a prerequisite for being a witness. And part of our human purpose, of our being God's stewards on Earth, is to be a witness to God and for God. By failing to be credible witnesses, extremists have defied their God-given purpose.

Closed, punitive, self-righteous religion is the real enemy of the good in religion, culture, and politics. That is where the most important intellectual, theological, religious, and political battle line exists today. What we need today is for American Muslims, Christians, Jews, and others to build a nationwide coalition of nonviolent moderates across religious lines to push for these overarching principles. We also need a worldwide coalition of nonviolent moderates across Muslim, Christian, Jewish, Hindu, Buddhist, and other religious communities to push for similar principles. The more such project-based coalitions we can build to address critical issues, the better off we all will be.

God's words in the Quran are as powerful today as they were when the Prophet first heard them. Repel evil with what is better "until the one whom you have enmity with is transformed into a passionate friend" (Quran 41:34).

Strategically, however, the challenge remains: How do we help expedite justice in today's world? The best answer, I believe, is to launch a principled doctrine of Islamic nonviolence reflecting the ultimate values of Islam, the Quran, and the Prophet. Muslims often ask, What would the Prophet do if he were alive today? I believe he would be an avid advocate of nonviolence, and that he would work for the establishment of a nonviolent "global movement of the moderates" across faith traditions.

The world witnessed and remembers the success of Gandhi's nonviolent struggle for Indian independence. Almost no one remembers his Muslim partner and colleague, Khan Abdul Ghaffar Khan, who became known as Badshah Khan. Khan taught, preached, and practiced nonviolence to his people, the Pashtuns, who lived, and still do live, in what is today the area straddling Pakistan and Afghanistan, and made a powerful case for nonviolence as a cardinal Islamic principle. "It is my inmost conviction," he said, according to Eknath Easwaran, "that Islam is '*'amal, yaqeen, mahabbah*'—selfless service, faith and love." By practicing nonviolence in the face of British violence, many of his people bravely faced death under British rule, and their nonviolent behavior eventually forced the British to transfer power to India.

Khan's work gives us a lens through which to understand events during 2011, when in Tunisia, Egypt, Bahrain, Yemen, Iran, and Syria many thousands, mostly the young, marched for reform or revolution chanting *silmiyya* (peacefully or nonviolently). *Silmiyya* is based on the same root, *slm,* from which the words *salaam* (peace) and *islam* are derived. Their call was for justice, and that they insistently demanded justice in the name of *silmiyya,* or nonviolence, is proof of Badshah's teaching that Islam is action that emanates from absolute faith, conviction, and love.

The world needs an Islamic nonviolent movement to partner with other faith groups also committed to nonviolence.

Cordoba House as a Tool for Fighting Extremism

Cordoba House, which became known as the "Ground Zero mosque," is based on this strategy of uniting nonviolent moderates against extremists. In order to battle extremism, nonviolent moderates of all faiths need concrete projects to work on together, so they can gain the experience of working with each other and discover what they have in common, combine their energies, and create that critical mass of focused spiritual power.

On May 5, 2010, a subcommittee of New York Community Board 1 welcomed and gave its unanimous approval to the establishment of Cordoba House, a community center in lower Manhattan. Then the firestorm hit. Islamophobic bloggers discovered Cordoba House, and soon mainstream, if highly partisan, outlets such as the *New York Post* and Fox News began pounding away at us. In spite of our trying to do the opposite, they accused us of being "insensitive" to the losses of the 9/11 families. The idea that the very religion which inspired the hijackers would establish a presence on "hallowed ground" was called an insult to the people who had died there, as well as to New Yorkers and all Americans. This was taking religious tolerance too far, they said; it was Muslims who had flown into the Twin Towers, so they should have the decency to stay away, far away.

The project became a key battleground in the global struggle between people advocating nonviolence and extremists. The media fanned Islamophobic flames throughout the election season of 2010 as politicians and pundits, commentators and demagogues, television hosts and bloggers uttered pronouncements on whether we should keep Cordoba House where we planned it or move it "a mile away" to some other site, Staten Island, say, or cancel the project altogether. I had to examine my own motives and those of my colleagues in pursuing this project. After a career spent trying to reduce tensions between Muslims and non-Muslims, it was ironic that I was being used as a tool to fuel those very tensions.

From the very beginning we had envisioned Cordoba House as a project that could help heal the wounds of 9/11. Instead, in a perfect example of the "big lie" of propaganda, we were accused of the precise opposite: dancing on the graves of Americans in a show of Islamic triumphalism. How offensive! Approximately sixty Muslims died in the attacks on the Twin Towers; thus we too lost members of our faith community. I had been a New Yorker for forty-five years, an American citizen since 1979. I was hurt and angered by the accusation.

We reached out to the 9/11 community, to the families that had lost loved ones that day. Perhaps the most important thing they said to me was that I should try to help bring about national healing of the wounds inflicted on 9/11 by speaking around the country about the vision and need for Cordoba House. I took their advice to heart. I concluded that I should not move Cordoba House just to satisfy some of the most bigoted voices in America and turn my back on my supporters. Where would "far enough" from Ground Zero be? As Clyde Haberman of the *New York Times* asked rhetorically, since twelve blocks (where my mosque is) was obviously acceptable, would four blocks also be acceptable, or eight? As the crisis intensified, I began, strangely enough, the worst and the best period of my entire life and vocation. On the one hand, my family and I, and my community, became the targets of a campaign of vilification and threats that made me fear for our physical safety. Cyberspace was even worse. To read the kinds of things people wrote—and still write—routinely on blogs about Islam, about Muslims, and about me took a strong stomach. It still does. We had experienced nothing like this in the aftermath of the 9/11 attacks nine years earlier.

Opponents of our initiative researched our supporters and called individual members of the foundation boards to insist that they withdraw funding from us. Our friends were threatened. One day, New York City Police Commissioner Raymond Kelly called my office to say that the Police Department had evidence of a "credible threat" against my life. I stayed away from the office for a while and lived at a friend's house. My BlackBerry rang nonstop; I had to get a second cell phone just to be able to have a conversation!

But here is the exciting thing: at the very same time, many thousands of New Yorkers, Americans from all fifty states, and people from forty-five countries (including Israel) on six continents sent us letters of support. They actively rallied to the cause of religious liberty and tolerance in a way they may never have done before; their letters and messages outnumbered the hate mail by a factor of 100 to 1. We were overwhelmed by their generosity. I received calls of support from around the world, including from the president of Turkey. The president of Indonesia had his ambassador to the United States fly to New York from Washington and deliver a letter to me strongly encouraging us to pursue our intention to make Cordoba House a truly multifaith center.

In the late summer of 2010 New Yorkers throughout the city hosted candlelight vigils and walks for religious tolerance. Jews, Christians, and nonbelievers met to plan support for our center. Rabbis at Rosh Hashanah services devoted their precious sermons on the New Year to the subject of the rights of Muslims to locate a mosque wherever they wished. When has such a thing ever happened in America? "To cave to popular sentiment would be to hand a victory to the terrorists," Mayor Michael Bloomberg said at an August 3 news conference with the Statue of Liberty in the background, "and there is no neighborhood in this city that is off limits to God's love and mercy." Rabbi Robert Levine of Congregation Rodeph Shalom said, "That mosque could serve . . . as an example of respect for all people and a model of interfaith cooperation and that's something that this city and this country needs desperately." But still the controversy boiled on.

Paradoxically, the controversy over the so-called Ground Zero mosque actually elevated America's reputation in the eyes of many Muslims. The fact that a U.S. president, the Jewish mayor of New York City, and Jewish and Christian religious leaders loudly and strongly supported our right to build the community center raised our country's standing in the Muslim world and validated decades of interfaith dialogue and friendships. A friend of mine in Egypt called me excitedly during the crisis to tell me that the English-language Egyptian newspaper *The Gazette* sported a front-page headline that read, "Obama OKs Mosque Plan Near Ground Zero." Muslims around the world could not believe this was happening in America!

It turns out that the folks in the 9/11 community were right. Americans all over the United States wanted to hear about Islam, about interfaith work, and about democracy in the Muslim world from a moderate American imam who became the most notorious Muslim in America. Americans wanted to heal, like the vast majority of 9/11 families themselves. For a year after the Cordoba House crisis started I was still fulfilling speaking engagements.

As the tenth anniversary of the attacks approached, I could see that with all the major events planned for the observance, wounds would be deliberately reopened, wounds that people hoped had healed. How could Muslims not be part of healing the wounds of 9/11? It was clear to me at the time, and remains so—and many non-Muslims agree with me—that because we Muslims are seen as part of what created 9/11, we need to be part of the resolution. That's what Cordoba House was designed to help accomplish: to provide a mechanism through which we can take some important steps toward the objective of national healing.

There are some people and organizations that do not want this healing to take place. There are extremists who want to keep the conflict going, even if they have to fabricate crises between Islam and the West. Why? There are opinion leaders, think-tank staffs, influential journalists and media figures, and politicians who appear to have a vested interest—political, financial, or ideological—in never resolving the conflict. They make their livelihood and their reputation from it. Even if the Taliban and all al-Qaeda affiliates disappeared tomorrow, they would tell us that the real enemy is still out there. For ideologues, facts never matter; they keep feeding extremists their lines because they need actors on the ground. Both the ideologues and the extremist actors are the common enemy of all of us of goodwill: Muslims, Jews, Christians, Buddhists, Hindus, atheists, and agnostics.

But the great majority of Americans do not want to believe that Islam is the enemy of the West; they do not believe that there is a *necessary* clash between Muslims and the United States. This is why our work is important. We therefore need to identify the ideologues and call them out, for they are working to undermine and betray the best interests of the United States of America, which lie in peaceful resolutions of international conflict. In August 2010 the Center for American Progress released a report that identified these ideologues, their academic supporters, their political supporters, and their funders. Don't these ideologues realize that by continually stirring the pot of religious and ethnic hatred, they put the security of the United States at risk, as well as the lives of those who wear the uniform of our country—as the secretary of defense reminded the Florida pastor? Hostile action breeds hostile reaction. Extremism on one side produces extremism on the other.

Cordoba House could be a beginning to breaking this cycle.

But we also need action on a much larger scale. The time has come for Muslims and Muslim leaders throughout the world to articulate, rally around, adopt, and implement an Islamic nonviolent approach and strategy: to ban the death penalty; to demonstrate that Islam is indeed a religion of peace and not of war; to combat and eliminate "Inquisitional Islam" (to use Christian language) or Khariji Islam (to use Islamic vocabulary) that the past half-century has produced.

I believe that as part of its program, the "global movement of the moderates" should embrace nonviolence theologically and practically and establish a global nonviolence coalition. Those of us outside the corridors of political power can call for the following:

- A coalition of nonviolent People of the Book—Muslims, Jews, and Christians—to bring peace to the Holy Land, to call upon the governments of Israel, Gaza, and the Palestinian Authority to push for a two-state solution. The Israeli and Palestinian economies would boom as peace is established in the region; business partnerships between Israelis and neighboring Arabs would spring up; and all would prosper. Israeli security would be guaranteed.

- A coalition of nonviolent Muslims and Hindus who call for India and Pakistan to return to their nonviolent roots and make peace with each other. With more than half a billion Muslims living in India, Pakistan, Bangladesh, and Afghanistan, the subcontinent needs massive collective pressure on behalf of ending Hindu-Muslim tensions and bringing peace to the region. The partnership of nonviolence between Badshah Khan and Gandhi that almost succeeded in solidifying Muslim-Hindu relations must be revived in a twenty-first-century version to bring about real peace between nations that are now nuclear powers. The risk to the world is too great to let this conflict fester.

The articulate, authentic, unified, worldwide voice of Islamic nonviolence can call for:

- Democratic regimes in the Muslim world and the Arab world: nonviolence between the rulers and the ruled;
- Women's rights: nonviolence between men and women and nonviolence in families;
- Freedom of thought: political, religious, social, and intellectual: nonviolence in mental and intellectual development;
- Freedom of the press: nonviolence toward journalists and the media;
- Freedom of religion: nonviolence toward religious minorities;
- Freedom of culture: nonviolence toward ethnic minorities;
- Individual dignity and the rule of law: nonviolence toward individuals and toward property.

It is my strongest hope that these principles will be taken up by and help guide the new global movement of moderates. Just imagine what such a movement could contribute to international dialogue and peacemaking!

6

ISLAM, THE STATE, AND POLITICS

At the World Economic Forum in Davos, Switzerland, in 2006 British Foreign Secretary Jack Straw wondered aloud why Americans were so hung up on church-state separation, adding something to the effect of "I appoint bishops!" Unlike Americans, for whom the phrase "separation of church and state" borders on political and religious dogma, the British have no such rule. The queen heads the Church of England, and in that capacity she appoints the Archbishop of Canterbury.

Nevertheless Great Britain has a complete *separation of religion and politics,* and the queen is also the "Defender of the Faith," who protects the freedom of religion and its exercise, which British citizens of all religious persuasions freely enjoy. We must distinguish, then, between the concept of church-state separation that many Americans consider a prerequisite for Western civilization, and that of the separation of religion and politics. It is precisely the *lack* of separation between religion and politics that has been the problematic issue in the history of religious communities, that Western countries have addressed in different ways. This distinction will help us see that there is more than one way to achieve a healthy relationship between institutions of political power and authority, on the one hand, and institutions of religious power and authority, on the other.

I believe that properly defining this relationship is perhaps the single most important unfinished business of the Muslim world. Pick a hundred Muslims at random and ask them if they believe in the separation of mosque (or religion) and state, and the likelihood is that most will say they do not. But as the British example shows, the issue is less the lack of separation between religion and state than the intrusion of politics into religion and of religion into politics that has sown confusion and fear among Muslims and non-Muslims.

"Islamic states" were created by Muslim political movements that lacked a clear idea of what that actually meant from an Islamic legal point of view. This has resulted in immense suffering and many miscarriages of justice. The 1947 partition of India and Pakistan resulted in the deaths of a half-million souls and has poisoned Hindu-Muslim relations ever since. Another partition, the creation of the Jewish State of Israel in 1948, fueled the growth of hostile attitudes toward Jewish minorities in Muslim-majority nations across the Middle East. Even the split of Sudan into the predominantly Muslim North and the mostly non-Muslim South in 2011 can be traced to the intrusion of Islam into Sudanese politics in the 1970s and 1980s. True, these divisions were also a consequence of colonialism and of the rise of authoritarian military and secular regimes as well as Islamic governments, but the historical verdict on the marriage of Islamic religious and political power cannot be judged generally successful in building prosperous and free societies.

Muslims demonstrating in Cairo's Tahrir Square in the wake of the Arab uprising of 2011, clamoring for Shariah law in Egypt, frightened secularists and the Coptic Christian minority. As public discourse became more extreme in that country, many feared imposition of a tyranny of the majority. Muslims all over the world also expressed concerns—which I shared—about what appeared to be evidence of a movement to make the entire country more religiously narrow and extremist. What is still needed in Egypt, and throughout the Muslim world, is a genuine understanding of what Islamic law really demands of a state and of good governance. The *New York Times* reported in 2011 that in Turkey, Egypt, Libya, and Tunisia, Muslim political activists were "confronting newly urgent questions about how to apply Islamic precepts to more open societies with very concrete needs." Turkey's prime minister made waves in Egypt and elsewhere in September 2011 by promoting the idea of a secular government led by an Islamic political party. And after Muammar Gaddafi's death in Libya in October 2011, the Western news was all atwitter when the head of the National Transitional Council of Libya announced that that country would be governed by Shariah.

Defining the Islamic State: The Shariah Index Project as a Step Forward

Until the early 1920s and the end of World War I, much of the Muslim world was ruled by local monarchs or Ottoman sultans. Since then there have been numerous movements to create Islamic states but insufficient clarity about what this means. Activists have founded Islamic political parties, movements, and even countries, but because these efforts originated with political activists (and, with the exception of Iran in 1979, not with Muslim religious scholars), they have traded in the currency of demographics or geography or political passion and power, and in the process the traditions of jurisprudence were often sidelined. There is growing recognition in the Muslim world that slogans from Islamic political parties are an insufficient basis for nation building. After all, where Islamic movements have achieved genuine political power, as in Iran and Gaza, the results have sometimes been contrary to Islam's ethical principles. So as more countries come under pressure to "Islamize" themselves, there is growing interest in developing an authentic, tradition-based, jurisprudential understanding of what an Islamic state ought to look like.

As an American Muslim who has lived in different societies around the world, Muslim as well as non-Muslim, I understand the way Muslim values have informed global political discourse and reform movements. I have witnessed firsthand the intersection between religion and politics and the need for a deeper, more dispassionate and systematic exploration of how Islam, politics, and the state inform each other.

In order to address this need I conceived the Shariah Index Project in 2003, with the goal of generating consensus among a group of jurists on defining what a twenty-first-century Islamic state looks like from the point of view of Shariah. We worked on creating an index to measure states' adherence to Shariah, and then rated Muslim-majority *and* non-Muslim-majority nations on how well they express the values of a true Islamic state.

The project finally launched in 2006. I discovered that many Muslim heads of government were seeking a set of criteria by which they could articulate their adherence to the principles of Shariah, mainly so they could present the results to their citizens. In almost every Muslim-majority nation there are political parties dedicated to establishing an Islamic state, but there is little or no consensus as to what such a state should look like. How, concretely and measurably, would an Islamic state differ from existing forms of government in the Muslim world or, for that matter, from the governments of mature Western democracies?

I brought together a working group of eminent Muslim scholars, jurists, and social scientists from Egypt, Iran, Turkey, Indonesia, Morocco, Bahrain, Palestine, Lebanon, Tunisia, Malaysia, Afghanistan, Pakistan, India, and the United States, and asked them to define the concept of an Islamic state from the point of view of Islamic law and to develop benchmarks for judging Muslim countries according to a modern understanding of classical Shariah.

Here is how they agreed to define an Islamic state. The rationale, or raison d'être, of an Islamic state lies in its acknowledgment of divine sovereignty, which is expressed concretely in two fundamental principles: the collective vice regency of the community and the supremacy of God's law (Shariah).

In the Quranic term *khalifa,* vice regent, is the idea that we humans are God's representatives on Earth, similar to the Christian notion that God meant people to be stewards of the Earth. The Prophet said, "My community will never collectively consent to a wrong" (Tirmidhi 1522). This *hadith* leads to the conclusion that *the collective will of human beings expresses what is right, and is therefore expressive of God's will.*

If we agree to this notion, then the next challenge is to establish a mechanism that can determine the collective will of a people. The majority of our scholars concluded that a representative democracy, which can determine the collective will of a people on a given matter, is the best contemporary method of determining God's will on the matter. We recognized, of course, that in any political system, including a democracy, certain groups or individuals try to skew the will of the people according to their own agendas, as has happened all too often in human history. That is why a healthy democracy needs effective checks and balances to ensure that such occurrences are minimized.

Any mechanism to determine the community's collective will would make use of principles of consultation (*shura*) in order to arrive at whatever level of consensus (*ijma*) a community believes is appropriate to the issue at hand: a plurality, simple majority, two-thirds majority, or even unanimity. (Consider the different levels of consensus in American institutions: simple majorities of Congress pass laws; a two-thirds majority of Congress is required to override a presidential veto; to convict on a criminal offense, juries must be unanimous.) Such mechanisms would need to be developed in a manner suitable to the community and its culture. Whether political leaders hold office, or are turned out of office, by appointment or election, they must have the consent of the governed (*bay'ah*), either of the entire population or by their legitimate representatives.

Human beings also need some overall sense of God's guidance and limits. Divine laws provide the moral framework of justice and of actions that must be prohibited, such as murder, theft, slander, adultery, and coercion of people's beliefs. Good governance must provide for people's needs that are the converse of each of these sins, which, according to God, are their rights. This is what is meant by the supremacy of God's law. God's law in an Islamic state is ideally represented through an economically and politically independent judiciary, which acts through courts to ensure justice and serves as a check on the legislative process to ensure that no law violates Shariah.

According to the scholars of the Shariah Index Project, the overarching purpose of an Islamic state lies in its "deliverables" or "performance indicators," as people say in the business world: to guarantee justice and the equality of all people under the law and to protect and further the fundamental rights of its citizens as described by the six objectives of Shariah:

- Life, which means national security and individual security. It includes health care and the ability to have food, shelter, and clothing at the most basic level.
- Religion, which means freedom of religious expression and government support of faith communities to practice their faith without government coercion.
- Property, which means material and financial sufficiency to provide for a good quality of life in all its aspects, as indicated in the other items listed here.
- Intellect, which means the ability to develop one's mind and intellectual pursuits and wisdom through education, including worldly, ethical, and moral knowledge.
- Family, which means the ability to marry and to satisfy human needs for emotional and physical companionship.

- Human dignity, which means the right to enjoy all the above and to live an honorable life free of slander or false accusation.

The scholars differed passionately on the need for a government to officially declare God as the Sovereign, or Islam as the state religion, or Shariah as the supreme law, and there were strong differences of opinion on the mechanisms or institutions by which these objectives could be achieved. These differences were understandable, as the scholars hailed from countries with political systems ranging from monarchies to republics, and from explicitly secular to proudly Islamic. But they unanimously agreed on the deliverables, on what Islamic states must provide their inhabitants. Despite disagreements about how to define the legitimacy or adequacy of specific political systems, they agreed that an Islamic state had to deliver justice, equality under the law, and, as best it could, the objectives of Shariah.

The Shariah Index Project has been a wonderful eye-opener for Muslims around the world, as the scholars involved, like many scholars of Islamic jurisprudence in the most important centers of Muslim learning today, believe that Shariah strongly supports what we now understand as human rights, gender equality, justice for the poor, and political democracy, among many other modern principles.

The Quran contains very specific demands from God about justice, about feeding and helping the poor, about protecting and educating orphans through their adulthood, when they can then take care of themselves, about the rights of women, about religious freedom and tolerance, and about human rights, most broadly conceived. In order to truly be an Islamic state, a country needs to pay close attention to these positive principles of Shariah, for a society's values and structure are determined most of all by its positive law *and not by its penal code*. The first responsibility of an Islamic state, in other words, is to provide justice to its citizens, not to punish its wrongdoers. And yet there have been states and movements calling themselves Islamic—the Taliban come to mind—that define their adherence to Shariah by their penal code (stoning and amputations) and dress code (burkas or head and face coverings for women and beards for men) above ethics and good governance. By engaging in systematic application of the six Shariah objectives in modern states, we measured the degree to which individual countries are compliant with the objectives of Shariah, or are *substantively Islamic* states: states meeting the objectives of Islamic law.

Why the United States Is Shariah-Compliant

In many ways the United States meets these Shariah objectives: it has a tradition of religious tolerance; it grants equality to people regardless of ethnicity or religious persuasion; women have equal rights and increasing roles at the higher levels of politics, society, and culture; it has a legal system that protects defendants' rights; there are checks and balances in place in the governmental structure; it has a social safety net that feeds, clothes, and shelters millions of poor and vulnerable Americans; the public and private educational system is accessible to the entire population; it has a public health system and a public retirement system. These are all ways of caring for the population either demanded or encouraged by Shariah. Of course the reality of drug use, the incarceration of a disproportionately large percentage of the African American population, persistent poverty and economic inequality in a wealthy country, high crime rates, and the sexual coarseness of much American popular culture all tend to lower the United States in this Shariah scoring.

But the similarities between America and the ideal Islamic state are philosophical as well as structural. The framers established a government whose worldview acknowledged a Creator. The first sentence of the American Declaration of Independence appeals to the authority of "the laws of nature and of nature's God"—the idea in Western law and philosophy of "natural law." Muslims speak of *din al-fitrah,* natural law (or natural religion; literally, the law or religion of nature), which the

Quran identifies with God's law (*din Allah*). To a Muslim ear, because God created nature, the laws of nature are obviously laws of God that He established. To speak of nature is to use secular or nontheistic language for what, for a Muslim, is de facto God's law. In other words, God created humans and the world with certain natural proclivities: natural law.

When, as a Muslim scholar, I look at the second, most renowned sentence in the Declaration of Independence—"We hold these truths to be self-evident, that all men are created equal, that they are endowed by their Creator with certain unalienable rights, that among these are life, liberty and the pursuit of happiness"—it is clear to me that the authors saw that as human beings created equally by God, we are all deserving of a law that takes human nature and human equality seriously. To be just, any law made by human beings must address the legitimate natural (God-given) needs of human beings; otherwise it cannot be natural, or God's law.

Note also the resemblance between "life, liberty and the pursuit of happiness" and the six objectives of Shariah. Life is a common objective in both. Liberty corresponds to the Shariah objective of dignity or honor. And what do people do to pursue happiness? Five centuries before Thomas Jefferson drafted the Declaration, Shariah scholars said that human pursuit of happiness lies in life, dignity, and freely practicing our choice of religion; in the acquisition of property (an earlier draft of the Declaration had "life, liberty, and property"); in seeking to marry our loved ones and raise a family; and in seeking intellectual stimulation, development, and education. The acknowledgment of God as sovereign continues into the Declaration's final paragraph, which appeals "to the Supreme Judge of the World for the Rectitude of our Intentions," and concludes with these words: "And for the support of this Declaration, with a firm Reliance on the Protection of divine Providence, we mutually pledge to each other our Lives, our Fortunes, and our sacred Honor."

As to the structural similarity between America and the ideal Islamic state, the founders established a government the legitimacy of which depended on the assent of its people: in the words of the Declaration, rulers derived "their just powers from the consent of the governed." In writing the Declaration the founders also had to enunciate a theory of when it would be possible or just to overthrow an illegitimate government. This is what they argued—in another parallel to Islamic legal theory of the state: "Whenever any Form of Government becomes destructive of these ends, it is the right of the people to alter or to abolish it."

Where America succeeded—and where the majority of modern authoritarian Muslim states have not—was in establishing an effective means of expressing the *collective vice regency of the community,* a representative democracy. Our elections produce a Congress intended to express the collective will of the people (when not thwarted by lobbies). Our judiciary is empowered to rule on the constitutionality of the laws it passes. This is the precise function of the judiciary in an Islamic state in which the judiciary is charged with ensuring that humanly enacted laws do not violate Shariah.

The fundamental point I want to make to Americans, Muslim and non-Muslim alike, and to Muslims around the world is that there is a profound congruence between the fundamental principles and objectives of Shariah, particularly concerning the laws of governance and the laws relating to worldly affairs, and the founding—and enduring—principles and structures of the United States of America.

Here in the United States, where political and religious pluralism are articles of faith, the ideal of one nation "under God"—as Abraham Lincoln (in the Gettysburg Address) and the Pledge of Allegiance put it and as our national motto, *E pluribus unum* (Out of many, one) expresses it—is the heart of the American social contract. It is completely compatible with Muslim values as well. In the Quran, after God describes having given Moses the Torah, and making Jesus and Mary a sign, he sums up by saying, "And indeed this, your religion, is one religion, and I am your Lord (Quran 23:52)—in other words, out of many, one. Although few on either side realize this, the truth is that Muslims here and abroad believe many of the same things Americans do.

Though a relatively young form of government in the sweep of world history, democracy represents a full expression of Abrahamic—and therefore Islamic—principles. This is how. The U.S. Constitution provides for checks on the power of each branch of government, which expresses the Shariah principle of *hisbah*. Equally important perhaps, the First Amendment to the Constitution, which prohibits establishment of a state religion (there it differs from an Islamic state), is intended to prevent the coercive practice of religion by a state and to ensure religious freedom, objectives also fundamental to Islam. After all, there is nothing about having a state religion that *necessitates* a coercive or exclusive attitude toward other religions, as is shown most prominently in the West, perhaps, by England, but also by Costa Rica, where Roman Catholicism is the state religion but other forms of worship may be freely exercised, and by Denmark, where the Lutheran Church is the state religion.

Despite the practice of some self-identified Islamic states today (such as Iran, Pakistan, and Saudi Arabia), the Quran states explicitly that "there shall be no compulsion in religion" (Quran 2:256) and that "He forged for each of us a law and a way" (Quran 5:48). Had God willed, He would have made us a people who all followed one way. But He gave us a variety of ways, presumably ways that would be suitable for each temperament, in order to test us in our capacity to truly fulfill what we have chosen of the way to worship Him. Had God willed, He would have made us all believers (Quran 5:48), but we are free to accept or reject God: that is the first test. Since it is God's will to have different faiths, God directs us how to address unbelievers: "To you your religion, and to me my religion" (Quran 109:6).

Since the Quran endorses Jews worshipping as Jews and Christians as Christians, it explicitly endorses the rights of religious pluralism, and until the last half of the twentieth century, most Muslim-majority countries protected religious minorities, including protecting a diversity of Islamic opinions regarding practice. Unfortunately in the past few decades an increasing movement to force all Muslims all over the world to adhere to only one interpretation is making us fail this tolerance test that God has given us.

Here I invite my American Muslim brothers and sisters to proudly claim their American identity. American law itself—no matter what the citizens of Oklahoma (who passed an amendment to the state constitution in 2010 prohibiting state courts from citing Shariah) and right-wing talk show hosts believe—expresses many of the objectives of Shariah and protects the delivery of these objectives far better than many Muslim-majority countries. Not only is the United States "Shariah-compliant" in all these ways; American Muslims fulfill the obligations of Shariah by virtue of our respect for American law and tradition. Let me emphasize this point, because it is so critically important for American Muslims and our non-Muslim neighbors in this country: *Shariah requires Muslim minorities to respect and follow the law of the land in which they live.* In other words, no matter what the State of Oklahoma insists upon legally, the United States is Shariah-compliant in important ways. American Muslims practice Shariah every day, from New York to California, from Minnesota to, yes, Oklahoma, just by complying with the law. So do non-Muslim Americans, day in and day out, every time they give thanks to God, every time they practice the Golden Rule, every time they worship God in church or synagogue or temple or meeting house, every time they are kind to strangers or their intimates, and every time they contribute to a charity.

On the other hand, in many Muslim countries there is a state religion, an "established religion," in the language of the Constitution, and religious freedom is increasingly compromised: one is free to practice only or mainly Islam or one interpretation of Islamic law. A friend of mine once told me about a multifaith group discussion with a high-level Moroccan government official in the 1990s. In response to a question about religious freedom, the official said, "Of course we have religious freedom in Morocco. Everyone is free to study the Quran!" In Saudi Arabia non-Muslim women must dress as though they are Muslims whenever they walk out the door, and the government flatly prohibits public worship of other religions. Is it any surprise, then, that many non-Muslims regard Islam as coercive and unprincipled, a faith of double standards? Because most Muslims consider Saudi Arabia their "holy land" it has enormous influence over what happens religiously in other Muslim-majority countries. Were the Saudi government to establish houses of worship for its more than a million Christian expatriates, it would strike a powerful international call for religious freedom, tolerance, and better understanding of Shariah and fulfill verse 22:40 of the Quran: "If God did not repel some people by others, cloisters, churches, synagogues and mosques in which God's name is much remembered [or hallowed and praised], would have been pulled down. And surely God will help those who help Him."

Shariah, Muslims, and Global Democracy

Just as there are many different forms of democracy in the world today, there can be many different types of Shariah-compliant Muslim states as well. American democracy is just one version. Great Britain still has a House of Lords and a monarch; many countries have a parliamentary system; and legal systems differ markedly. New democracies in Muslim-majority countries will create their own kinds of democracy as well. Some might go the way of constitutional monarchies; others may become republics.

To an extent unappreciated by most of the world, Shariah has much to say about the good governance of Muslim and indeed all societies. The remarkable demonstrations comprising the Arab uprising of 2011—from the revolutions in Tunisia and Egypt and Libya to the uprisings and demonstrations in Bahrain, Yemen, Syria, and Jordan—may have been the first visible proof to non-Muslims that

Muslims have long held the same desires for freedom and democracy as everyone else in the modern world. The fact that for the greater part of the past thousand years many Muslim-majority countries have been ruled by dynasties only indicates their resemblance to most countries and empires for most of that time—and has been cause for criticism and lament by Muslim scholars and activists, many of whom contend that there has been no truly Islamic state since the time of the Prophet and his immediate successors in Medina.

For its part, the West colonized most of the countries with large Muslim populations—such as Indonesia, Egypt, Iran, Sudan, Nigeria, Algeria, Morocco, Iraq, Afghanistan, and India (before there was Pakistan)—and preferred to deal with authoritarian postcolonial leaders in these countries to ensure compliance with foreign policy in waging the cold war. While Westerners, perhaps especially Americans, casually assume that Muslims abroad are content to be ruled by dictators, the reality is that during the second half of the twentieth century the United States often threw its weight overtly or covertly toward friendly strongmen with little appetite for democracy, such as Egypt's Hosni Mubarak, Shah Mohammad Reza Pahlavi of Iran, and Suharto of Indonesia. To then blame these monarchies and dictatorships on the allegedly backward or brainwashed Muslim masses they oppressed is unfair, at the very least. You can imagine how Egyptians, Iranians, and Indonesians react to such condescending, historically ignorant accusations.

Muslims around the world have no more and no less to apologize for than any other peoples that have lived under despotic authoritarian regimes for long stretches of time: the hundreds of millions of people constituting the USSR and the Soviet bloc until 1989, Cubans under Castro, black South Africans under apartheid until 1994, Chileans under Allende, Burmese under the generals, and North Koreans under Kim Jong-il. As our own Declaration of Independence observed in 1776, "all experience hath shown that mankind are more disposed to suffer, while evils are sufferable, than to right themselves by abolishing the forms to which they are accustomed." But the Quran promises everyone the right to live a life of dignity, and Islamic law has elaborated a philosophy of political leadership over the centuries that most Americans would recognize and find congenial. It is about providing justice.

The concept of justice includes a number of corollaries. Legitimate government must value truth, protect the weak from the strong, and have the consent of the governed. And the people who consent to be governed may not be coerced. When Abu Bakr, the first caliph and closest companion to the Prophet Muhammad, accepted the role of ruler of the people of Medina, he said:

> I have been given authority over you, and I am not the best of you. If I do well, help me; and if I do wrong, set me right. Sincere regard for truth is loyalty and disregard for truth is treachery. The weak amongst you shall be strong with me until I have secured his rights, God willing; and the strong amongst you shall be weak with me until I have wrested from him the rights of others, if God will. Obey me as long as I obey God and His Messenger. But if I disobey God and His Messenger, you owe me no obedience.

In comparison, think of the elections that so-called democratic rulers win by 90 percent, or the balloting that takes place under the armed surveillance of a dictator. The "winners" announce their overwhelming victory, which could only have happened by coercing the governed into giving their consent. This is not real consent.

Rulers must stay faithful to divine prescriptions; when they do not, those they rule are released from their obligations. Political leadership involves a mutual relationship between rulers and the ruled. The ruled owe allegiance only to rulers who remain faithful to a higher law and do not place themselves above the law. At the same time, elected leaders' qualifications for office should be based not on how religious they are, but on how capable they are of protecting the rights of the governed and providing justice. You see here that leaders can be neither complete secular pragmatists (unless they also follow divine law) nor complete religious idealists (unless they can show tremendous practical competence). And because no government is infallible, they must allow themselves to be checked, as the U.S. Constitution provides for checks and balances between the three branches.

These ideas come directly out of the Quran, the *Hadith,* and centuries of Islamic scholarship and jurisprudence. Millions of Muslims who never dreamed that their religion took such powerful positions in favor of legitimate, democratic government find these ideas powerfully liberating. We have seen some of the results of their commitment in the streets of Cairo, Teheran, Tunis, and Daraa, Syria.

You may recall the moving footage and many stories, in the midst of the 2011 Egyptian revolution against the authoritarian Mubarak regime, of Muslims and Coptic Christians taking turns protecting each other from attacks by the police during their respective prayers in Tahrir Square. What an image: demonstrations for democracy in a majority-Muslim country in which activists stood ready to protect their allies and friends of other faiths as they struggled together on behalf of common dreams. I know that this fragile alliance has frayed since the heady early days of the revolution, but it has done so because extremists have whipped up public sentiment in both communities. And yet such an alliance is possible and must be sustained.

The danger is that in the rush by Islamic political parties and their supporters to establish Shariah law, these nascent democracies may make the same mistakes as the Taliban and countries like Pakistan and Nigeria, believing that the way to establish Islamic statehood is by focusing first of all on the penal code, forcing people to wear their religion on their sleeves. If someone suggested that by punishing criminals the way Americans do, forcing people to dress as Americans do, and worshipping in American Protestant churches, a U.S.-style democracy would be thereby automatically created, you would wonder about his sanity. Yet several so-called Islamic states—the Taliban most egregiously of all—have done precisely that: focused on punishing people according to a misunderstanding of Shariah; forcing men to grow beards and women to wear burkas; denying women education; and forcing people to perform certain acts of worship. And they actually believed that they had thereby established an Islamic state!

We gain a broader understanding of Islam and the state, and the scholarly and political debates over the nature of an Islamic state, by remembering the Shariah ruling that minorities are to respect and follow the law of the land in which they live. This Shariah ruling is based on the Prophet's instructions to his followers whom he sent to live in Abyssinia (modern Ethiopia), then ruled by a Christian king. Muslims are still a minority in Ethiopia fourteen centuries later, and at no time has there ever been any effort or any suggestion by Muslim scholars anywhere in the world that Ethiopian Muslims should force Shariah law upon the rest of Ethiopia. Based on this history, Muslim scholars also said that there is no requirement (in the Quran or the *Hadith*) for Muslims to establish an Islamic state. The only requirement is that when they are in office, they should rule justly.

The fundamental principle of legitimate government, according to Shariah, is that it be just, that it abide by God's law—not that it proclaim itself Islamic or secular. In one of his best-known sayings on the importance of justice in defining good governance, the fourteenth-century scholar-jurist Ibn Taymiyya declared, "Allah will raise up [or establish] the just state even though it is unbelieving [*kafirah*], and will not raise up the unjust state even though it is Muslim."

In order to be a genuine Islamic state, a government needs to deliver justice to its people by helping them achieve the six objectives of Shariah: protecting and furthering the development of human life, dignity, religion, property, family, and intellect. As the heady days of the Arab uprising—with its own declarations of independence and freedom from unjust rulers—give way to the more prosaic business of constructing constitutions faithful to the deepest concerns of Islamic law, I hope and pray that the architects of these new legal systems will take lessons from countries where the state religion protects all citizens' rights to speak and study and assemble and worship as they please. It would be hard to find an action more opposed to God's explicit commandments in the Quran that there shall be no coercion in religion than the forcing of the worship of believers in faiths other than Islam into hiding, or treating those believers as criminals. In a true Islamic state, a truly just state, human beings are freed to realize their potential—not made prisoners of an authoritarian majority.

Conclusion
ISLAM THE AMERICAN WAY

From Muslims in America to American Muslims

One way to look at American Muslim life and culture in the early decades of the twenty-first century is as an enormous painting of myriad individual vignettes. There are certainly common patterns among those vignettes, but there are also many different vignettes within a single city. American Muslims are, after all, a cross-section of the global Muslim community: in one city alone we can have Turkish, Albanian, Egyptian, West African, Pakistani, Bangladeshi, and African American mosques. Most of these religious communities have coalesced around the ethnic and cultural characteristics immigrants brought from their home countries.

But Muslims in America are in the process of developing an American Islamic cultural and institutional identity. We are evolving from being immigrant Muslims in America—whether in ethnic or religious enclaves—to being American Muslims. (These issues are of course far more important for Muslims who have immigrated to the United States in recent years than for African American Muslims, who have been Americans and Muslims for generations.) But we are doing so accidentally and unconsciously, when we need to be much more deliberate and intentional as we integrate our laws into this country while remaining fully in keeping with the historicity and continuity of Islamic legal thought.

We can predict, for example, that the second and third generations of Muslim immigrants in particular will want both to be connected to their faith *and* to fit into American culture. I know a young Indian man, for example, who feels like a misfit when he visits the mosque his father helped establish in Queens, New York, because, he says, it seems to have been airlifted wholesale from Gujarat, a state in Western India. Everything about it, from the way it is run to the way people behave and the way it is decorated inside, makes him feel alien and uncomfortable. All religions have had to go through these transitional moments.

American Muslims read the same Quran as the rest of the world's 1.6 billion Muslims. We worship the same God, pray identically, fast during the month of Ramadan, contribute to our community, and dream of going on the *hajj*. At the same time, as countless millions migrate from one side of the world to another, Muslims not only find themselves in new countries or cultures; they also find themselves living and working and worshipping next to Muslims from very different countries and cultures, often lumped together by their host culture.

Over the past forty-five years, as I have watched Islam grow and develop in this country, I have pondered the experience of previous migrant, immigrant, and faith groups as a guide to the future of American Muslims. Irish Catholics had to face brutal discrimination and the occasional riot simply because they were Irish and Catholic in an overwhelmingly Protestant country, most of whose founders were of English origin. Eastern European Jews confronted religious discrimination from Catholics and Protestants and ethnic discrimination from a population drawn mostly from Northern and Western Europe. Asians, Mexicans, and Latinos have suffered ethnic, racial, and linguistic discrimination, oftentimes written into American laws. African Americans, of course, faced the most brutal conditions of all immigrants: literally stolen from their native lands (where some 10 to 15 percent were Muslims) and sold to slave traders, they endured two and a half centuries of slavery, another century of legal peonage, and all of the residue of institutional racism. All of these groups worked for nothing or low wages in dreadful conditions and contributed mightily to building the American economic colossus of the nineteenth and twentieth centuries.

To varying degrees, all of these groups have now become integrated into American society. They have produced presidents, senators, Supreme Court justices, billionaires, professional athletes, university presidents, bankers, entertainers, artists, and Nobel Prize winners.

We will be no different. The number of well-known American Muslims is already substantial and growing, particularly in the past couple of decades. The list includes a Nobel Prize winner in chemistry (Ahmed Zewail), the editor-at-large of *Time* magazine (Fareed Zakaria), the supermodel Iman, comedians (Aasif Mandvi, Dave Chappelle), numerous boxers (Muhammad Ali, Eddie Mustafa Muhammad), professional basketball players (Rasheed Wallace, Shaquille O'Neill), and football players (Ahmad Rashad, Ryan Harris), jazz musicians (Art Blakey, Yusef Lateef) and pop musicians (Ice Cube, Mos Def), and two members of the U.S. House of Representatives (Keith Ellison, Andre Carson).

I love that there are Muslim pro athletes, so that our young people (and the occasional older one as well) can have the same experience some of my African American, Latino, and Jewish friends did as children, rooting for Jackie Robinson and Willie Mays in New York, Roberto Clemente in Pittsburgh, or Sandy Koufax in Los Angeles. When Cassius Clay publicly embraced Islam in 1964 and became Muhammad Ali, he sent a thrill through the Muslim world. Hundreds of millions of people, including stolid academic scholars and men and women who had never taken any interest in sports and who considered boxing a violent and un-Islamic sport, suddenly became boxing fans!

American Muslims do not hail from any one country. Even more diverse than Catholic or Eastern Orthodox immigration in the late nineteenth century (from Italy, Poland, Germany, Croatia, Greece), Muslims come to America from Turkey, Pakistan, Indonesia, China, Iraq, Iran, Senegal, India, Guinea, Nigeria, Afghanistan, Somalia, Ethiopia, Egypt, Jordan, Lebanon, India, Malaysia, Bosnia, Yemen, Bangladesh, Morocco, and the Philippines—among many other countries. We are a cross-section of Muslims from all over the world.

One of the questions facing us as a multiethnic community here in America is whether we will become a Muslim melting pot. Love knows no borders. If people have the opportunity to meet and live and study and work alongside each other, they will develop friendships, sometimes deep ones, and even romantic relationships across ethnic, racial, religious, and cultural lines. We religious leaders have to be adequately prepared to deal with the reality that is already upon us and will only intensify in years to come.

A Muslim girl wants to marry a Jewish boy. An Indian Muslim boy wants to marry a Hindu girl he met at college. All the parents are confused and upset; traditional immigrant fathers tend to issue rigid pronouncements, while the mothers work harder to keep their families from being torn apart. I see this happening in my office, where I meet with a Turkish girl who immigrated to the United States with her parents. She has met an Afghan boy in college and fallen in love with him; now they want to get married. Both are Muslims, so religion is not an issue here. But her father insists that she has to marry a Turk, so she has come to me for help. We Muslims could use our own version of *West Side Story*.

When these young people come to us at the Society for Muslim Advancement, or to me as an imam, they are looking for more than a statement of what is right and what is wrong. If I tell this young woman that because she and her intended are both Muslims there is no religious issue, and that's that, I haven't helped her deal with her father.

In most traditional cultures, a daughter's marriage requires the permission of her father or guardian, and because Muslim legal scholars recognized the law of custom as an acknowledged source of law, most schools of law adopted the pre-Islamic cultural practice of requiring the agreement of a woman's guardian. If I want to be simply Shariah-correct, I could tell her that according to the Hanafi school of legal interpretation, which is the dominant school in Turkey and Afghanistan, she has the right to marry without the permission of her father. But the real battle here is between cultural practices and what kind of a life a couple will have if cut off from their parents.

In American society, the cultural norm is for parents not to get in the way of love. So the Islamic jurisprudential formula would conclude that in America we should let the lovers have their way. However, explaining the legal reasoning behind such a position is often too abstract for the parties involved. And simply to cite the Shariah (legal) position—which sides with American culture against traditional culture—does not help them either.

In practice we engage these families in a process and try to figure out a way by which we can reconcile them; after all, the father does not want to lose his daughter, and the daughter does not want to reject her family's culture or origins. In our experience immigrant mothers are often the more helpful parent in moving toward consensus. We help the family get there. At the time of this writing, it looks as though this family is heading toward a reconciliation.

So many situations just walk in the door. Instead of saying, "Muslim women cannot marry non-Muslim men. Forget about it, and get out of my office," a position held by many imams in America, especially foreign-trained ones, Daisy and I try to be sympathetic, to understand the particulars. I feel sympathetic because I remember how in my own life, at different points in my youth I had crushes and fell in and out of love with women of different ethnic and religious backgrounds. I myself have experienced marriage and divorce across religious and ethnic lines. As a result I can sympathize with people with these problems. I understand the challenges they are confronting. And I wish I had had someone to help me navigate those emotionally intense moments in my life in ways that were true to my emotions, my culture, my religion, and, perhaps most important, my long-term happiness and emotional fulfillment.

Our global future gets hammered out in such individual relationships and in the offices of clergy and therapists all over this country. We American Muslims may even be leading the way toward the multiethnic future, particularly in New York City and other large urban centers. I have congregants whose parents are Irish and Arab, Pakistani and American, Sudanese and American, African American and Chinese, Bosnian and Senegalese, and Bangladeshi and Greek American. How can we not celebrate this blending of cultures, this great adventure that our young people are pioneering?

That is why at the Society for Muslim Advancement we have worked so hard on supporting interfaith marriages in a manner that respects both religious traditions. We have learned that it is not enough to give young people (or older people) in love legally valid and emotionally irrelevant advice. We must deal with the powerful emotional attachments people have about issues of culture and the genuine psychological, emotional, and familial realities people are facing as they think about marrying outside of their home culture, home country, or home religion. It is why we developed a process by which a Muslim woman *can* marry a non-Muslim man with the blessings of both religious traditions, cultural traditions, families, and communities.

We need to figure out what is relevant to us as Muslims, and what is less so.

When young and impressionable Muslims see themselves constantly presented as terrorists, these images may become self-fulfilling prophecies. Instead they need to see versions of themselves in the popular culture that they can look up to. In order to combat such misperceptions, through the Cordoba Initiative I have commissioned film scripts and urged American entertainment and news media to develop programming that depicts Muslims like any other American religious or ethnic community and shatters stereotypes of Muslims as uneducated, sexist terrorists.

In January 2007, at a meeting to discuss U.S.-Muslim relations, former secretary of state Madeleine Albright suggested that my wife and I produce a Muslim version of *The Cosby Show,* a program that played an important role in changing racial stereotypes and in inspiring African Americans with positive values of family, upward mobility, and the importance of higher education. The idea was spoofed on Jon Stewart's *The Daily Show* as "The Qu'osby Show." I agreed to be "interviewed" by the comedian Aasif Mandvi, even though I knew that few "interviewees" escape unscathed from Mandvi's humor, because I thought it was worth the risk to show Muslims and non-Muslims alike that a Muslim cleric can participate in American popular culture and not take himself over-seriously.

Too many religious professionals, in my view, make the mistake of trying to stand outside of the life most people live, implying their superiority to "normal life." But the Prophet Muhammad himself lived a fully engaged human life. He married, he divorced, he had children, and he suffered from the death of his infant children. He married a Jewish woman and a Copt from Egypt. There is a report that his Coptic wife, Maria, died while clutching the Bible to her chest.

In addition to being a prophet and spiritual leader, he was a political leader, the mayor of Medina, commander-in-chief, and chief judge. When Muslims talk about his *sunna,* his life, his practice, that is what makes him so relevant, and still relevant, to more than a billion Muslims today. In one *hadith* the Prophet says that scholars are the heirs of the prophets (Tirmidhi 3449). In other words, Muslim scholars and imams have a responsibility to exhibit this worldly aspect of the Prophet's life, so as to be able to help bring their communities to authentic worship of God by their counsel, their sermons, and their writings. The prophets were not mere theoreticians and academics; they were activists par excellence. Imams and scholars who have not walked in the shoes of their followers too often cannot relate to their problems and their lives.

This is why American Muslims must invest in creating our own, American, homegrown scholars and imams, who have experienced what members of their communities are going through and can provide genuine and meaningful help and leadership. We need imams and scholars who know the cultural influences: who the rappers are, who is playing in the Super Bowl, and that *American Idol* is a TV show and not a god for people to worship. If our imams all come fully formed from the majority-Muslim world, they will have only theoretical, not experiential, knowledge of what their congregations are dealing with on a daily basis. We must make more room for homegrown imams in our mosques.

I know that the American demographic transformation worries a lot of people of good faith. They are concerned that their streets and shopping centers and supermarkets will no longer be recognizable, that more and more Americans will speak English with a foreign accent, that unfamiliar smells will waft across food courts, that strange customs will change the calendar, odd forms of dress will shake up their social expectations, and unpleasant music will blare out of radios.

At one level they are absolutely right: these changes are not only coming; they are well under way. We are smack in the middle of one of those culturally transformative eras that have periodically reshaped American society, culture, and politics, most recently about a century ago, in the several decades leading up to World War I. Millions of Southern and Eastern Europeans, mostly Catholics and Jews, gave an entirely new flavor to most of our great cities. New words, images, foods, pastimes, and patterns of worship entered America's religions, vocabulary, leisure, and diet. And in a generation or two they were embraced by the larger culture—they had become American.

At the same time, immigrants themselves struggled (and struggle today) to adapt to American society, shedding much of their traditional dress, language, hairstyles, and customs. These are the patterns that will govern Latino, Asian, and, as we will see, Muslim adaptation to American culture.

Organized Islam in America

In most Muslim-majority countries, Islam is an "established" religion, in the language of the Declaration of the Independence. There is a Ministry of Religious Affairs, sometimes called the Ministry of Religious Trusts (*awqaf*), that is responsible for running all the mosques in the country: their administration, maintenance, personnel, and often the types of sermons allowed.

In the United States, on the other hand, where we have separation of church and state, Islam is completely decentralized, and Muslims are free to say what they wish. But because we Muslims are so diverse, we have as yet been unable to forge denominational structures comparable to the Union of Reform Judaism, or the Archdiocese of New York, or the National Baptist Convention. Attempts began as early as the 1960s to establish a central organization of Muslims in America, but because of the rapid growth of immigrants from very different cultural backgrounds, such efforts have rarely been successful beyond a local level or a brief period of time. Here in America we are more democratic, more independent, and therefore more chaotic. And since roughly two-thirds of American Muslims are either immigrants or of recent immigrant origin, mosques have tended to import imams from their home countries and look to home country sources for their religious understanding, practice, and custom. Although an imam's sermon might get him fired (as a rabbi's, priest's, or minister's can) by his congregation, there is no religious hierarchy setting limits on what he can say.

In practice, this democratic reality means that each mosque is on its own in terms of fund-raising, administration, staffing, and programs—even when it celebrates our holidays! Since Ramadan begins with the sighting of the first crescent of the new moon in the ninth month, some mosques begin the holiday based on when the moon is first sighted in their congregants' home country; others base the sighting in Mecca, and still others use the United States. These dates can differ by a day or two, and it is not unusual to see New York City Muslims celebrate their holidays on as many as three different days!

Because American culture is so egalitarian in so many different ways, including in the workplace and the household, American Muslim women (like American Christian and Jewish women before them) are playing an increasingly important role in their mosques and communities and in shaping the contours of Islam in America, as they seek to fulfill their own religious needs and to develop their own spirituality. In a self-reinforcing circle, their increasing participation in mosques is making mosques more gender-egalitarian institutions. As a result women are pioneering an American Islamic culture in which they are playing more important roles. In the summer of 2011 Daisy gave a lecture in a mosque in the Bronx run and populated by French-speaking West Africans from Mali, Senegal, and the Ivory Coast. Women made up about half the audience. On Long Island there is a mosque not only with women members of the board, but with a woman president of the board, which is empowered to hire and fire the imam. Ingrid Mattson, the Canadian-born first female president of the Islamic Society of North America, owed her selection to this egalitarian spirit.

Halal Food: A Cuisine?

Pizza and bagels are just two examples of immigrant foods becoming part of the larger culture's diet. But this is a much larger story, one that continues to this day. At the turn of the twentieth century native-born Americans loudly complained about the strong smells and flavors of cooking that used large amounts of garlic, olive oil, onions, and pungent cheeses. Italians were derided as "garlic-eaters," and in an era when it was common to eat one's lunch or supper in a movie theater some owners banned Italian sandwiches.

Nowadays immigrants are again remaking the American diet, and many of those immigrants—from South Asia and China and Africa and the Middle East—are Muslims. Their food is spicier—in very different ways—than most Italian food (especially the watered-down American versions), and they have made cities like New York a real mecca for international food. But we still hear of many an American neighbor complaining of the strong smell of fried Indian spices or an Indonesian neighbor's frying shrimp paste.

Islam and mosques can play an important role here as well. One reason I went to religious meetings and gatherings in the 1970s, before becoming an imam, was because they were some of the only places I could find excellent Indonesian or Malaysian food. To this day my brother-in-law attends a certain mosque because he claims the congregation serves the best biryani in New York. That would not have been much of a claim in New York twenty years ago. Today, given the competition, these are almost fighting words. I conducted the wedding of a young Italian American man to a Muslim woman of Indian origin; the groom spoke of his mother-in-law's biryani with sparks in his eyes nearly equaling those he had for his bride!

Is there anything in the Quran about biryani? Not directly, but the story of the Children of Israel being dissatisfied with a constant menu of manna from heaven and asking Moses for the cucumbers, garlic, onions, and lentils of Egypt makes the point (Quran 2:61). Human beings eat several times a day; every time they plant a vegetable garden or shop for or make a meal they are making cultural decisions (and sometimes religious ones as well) that affect their families, their neighbors, and their surrounding culture. Here is a point at which we immigrant Muslims can simultaneously enter, enrich, and embrace American culture.

A young Muslim friend told the story of how she and her coworkers were discussing what to have for lunch—Chinese, Indian, Italian, pizza, deli—when one of her colleagues said, "Let's eat *halal*!" To a Muslim *halal* is not a cuisine; rather, it is meat that is "kosher" for Muslims to eat. But her story shows how, with the plethora of food carts on so many New York City street corners advertising *halal* food, Muslims have already made a culinary impact on an entire generation of New Yorkers. I understand that there's a *halal* food cart on the corner of Fifty-third Street and Sixth Avenue that has achieved such gourmet status that there is a line of customers going around the block even at 3 a.m.!

As long as a meal does not involve pork or alcohol, it is permitted. Consider the American Thanksgiving. There is nothing in the Quran or the *Hadith,* obviously, on the subject of this quintessentially American holiday, but one of God's attributes, or names, is "the Thankful" (*Al-Shakur*). The core meaning of the Arabic word *kufr* (disbelief in God) is "ingratitude," and one of God's frequent criticisms of humans in the Quran is "Little are you grateful!" Since giving thanks, expressing thanksgiving, is such a positive value, a holiday devoted to such feelings must be a positive good. This American tradition devoted to thanking God is a very Islamic action, so Thanksgiving can and should be considered not only an American but also a thoroughly Muslim holiday.

Moreover the protection and promotion of family is one of the six objectives of Shariah. Since Thanksgiving is such a family-oriented holiday, I think it is important for American Muslims to participate fully in the ritual, turkey and all—and most American Muslims do. We may have Egyptian salads, or hummus instead of cranberry sauce—my mother preferred to make a *burghul* (bulgur dish) or rice instead of cornbread stuffing—and the pumpkin pie might be a little spicier than most Midwesterners are used to (it might even be an African pumpkin soup), but I assure you that it will be recognizably a Thanksgiving feast. Because it so deeply expresses Islamic values, I believe strongly, based on legal teachings, that the imams who argue that Thanksgiving is un-Islamic (because it is new to their traditions or because they fear cultural assimilation in America) are doing our community a disservice.

While we are at it, I can think of no reason why we Muslims cannot adopt the cookouts and picnics associated with Memorial Day and Labor Day as well. Each of these holidays, insofar as they still have serious content, are perfectly compatible with Muslim emphases on remembrance of the fallen and justice for workers. And as for the barbecue, we need hardly be limited to hamburgers and *halal* hot dogs. You should try my mother's hamburgers, for which she mixes cracked coriander seeds into the ground meat. Across the Muslim world lamb, mutton, goat, chicken, and fish make tasty *kebabs* (originally an Iranian word), whether the spices come from Tunisia or Turkey or Afghanistan. An American friend of ours raved about "those chicken sausages" when he had Pakistani-style chicken kebabs Daisy made for dinner recently.

Raising Muslim Children

Imam Ali, the Prophet's son-in-law and the fourth caliph, said in one of his most profound aphorisms, "Rear your children for a time different from your own." This is the perennial challenge of every religion. I remember when I first came to America, the rallying cry was "Modernity!" How were the ancient religions of Judaism, Christianity, and Islam dealing with the challenges of modernity? The truth is that religious communities have never been entirely static. Children have always faced a time different from their parents'. Now, however, the world is on the move at such a speed that many more of us must raise our children for a time *and a place* different from our own. That is what a "different time" means in practice. So now we join every religion in history in figuring out what are our eternal principles, and how we can express them in practice in a new time and a new context. Even God amended His own laws in different times and different contexts.

Who are we to stay stuck in the culture and customs and practices of our grandparents?

The hardest task for immigrant parents in a cultural and religious minority is to raise their children so they both embrace their new culture and do not completely reject that of their parents and grandparents. How can we Muslim parents be true to ourselves and our children, true to our religion, and true to the surrounding culture we now call home?

Inevitably immigrant parents will find their children's English-language skills outstripping theirs. Children's command of slang, of popular culture, of American customs and practices, sports and music, television and video games will quickly be so far beyond their parents' that generational tensions are inevitable and predictable.

Fortunately the world's most popular sport is probably the fastest growing sport in America, so we can encourage our children to play soccer secure in the knowledge that they will not be considered strange or foreign. I cannot emphasize too strongly how important it is for us to encourage our girls and young women to throw themselves into athletics. Sports is among the quickest ways to integrate into American society, but it represents much, much more. Everyone who studies the effects of girls' and women's sports finds that participants do better in school, have stronger self-esteem, and tend to value themselves independently of what boys and young men think of them. They also eat more healthfully and grow up healthier because of diet and exercise. They have less time to engage in unstructured "hanging out"—one of the more dangerous temptations for teenagers. Because they have higher self-esteem and self-confidence, athletic girls and young women are less vulnerable to the sexual pressure exerted by adolescent boys and young men, and are far less likely to become pregnant as teens, a problem I see increasingly even where I grew up, in Malaysia. And they are less likely to be tempted by alcohol, smoking, and drugs. Yes, even young Muslims are tempted by alcohol, and the sooner we adults realize it, the better.

There are real benefits of acculturation in sports for boys as well. I especially loved the August 2010 report in the *New York Times* about the high school football teams in Dearborn, Michigan (which have a very high percentage of Muslim students) that ran practices from 6 to 11 p.m. in one case, and from 11 p.m. to 4 a.m. in another, so that the young athletes could observe Ramadan's fast without dehydrating. What could be more American than high school football, and what is more Muslim than fasting during Ramadan? That's one example of what I call American Islam.

What about social life? No one would expect young American Muslim men or women to not attend parties or social functions with members of the opposite sex. The Quran is of course silent on the subject of hip-hop music, no matter how much many parents wish it were not, but a striking number of very well-known rappers are in fact Muslims. Muslim young (and not so young) people need not be prohibited from socializing with their non-Muslim friends who frequent bars or restaurants serving alcohol. They may find that being one of the few in their social set who does not drink gives them a certain popularity and cachet; it certainly protects young men and women from the extreme silliness and boorish behavior their non-Muslim friends frequently regret the following day, especially when the documentary evidence starts appearing on Facebook. It may also protect their friends from being tempted to drive cars under the influence of alcohol.

Our responsibility as American Muslims is to adapt our religion to American cultural norms. We need to help our young people fit into their schools and colleges and neighborhoods and social and cultural organizations. We need to make a conscious effort to do what our ancestors did: to adapt to this culture rather than make impossible demands on it. We need to encourage conversations within our communities about which cultural trappings are essential to our genuine religious identity and which are not, so that we are not simply raising culturally Senegalese or Turkish or Iranian Muslim children but are raising *culturally American and religiously Muslim* children in the United States.

No matter what fundamentalist and extremist voices abroad tell us about how we are "supposed" to act in the United States, our past Islamic heritage and historical tradition was to adopt our host cultures and adapt to them. For Muslims in America, our challenge is to make Islam an American religion. We will do that by raising children who will live as American Muslims for a time different from our own, living Islam "the American way."

Moving the Mountain

In the past half-century our 1,400-year-old faith has suffered twin assaults: extremism from within and demonization—Islamophobia—from without. For the world's 1.6 billion Muslims, as well as for the entire Western world, these assaults, which fuel each other, have created massive and devastating consequences: wars, terrorist attacks, millions of refugees, millions of deaths, cultural impoverishment, and widespread hatred and fear. That is the bad news.

The good news is that Muslims all over the world are now attempting to reclaim Islam from those who would make it the enemy of the West and the enemy of modern, moderate, just, open, egalitarian, and tolerant societies. These Muslims are fully engaged in the effort to move the mountain of extremism and hostility out of their way. As I travel around the world I see that most Muslims want a better relationship with the West, and with America in particular. And as I travel the United States I see that Muslims and non-Muslims are looking for help reconciling American and Muslim values, and many of them are influencing even their traditional homelands.

American technology, popular culture, corporations, and values have reshaped the world, including the Muslim world, over the past century. Muslims around the globe have responded, sometimes ideologically, sometimes religiously, sometimes politically, and sometimes violently, to what they have seen as a Western, and now a particularly

American, incursion into their world. American Muslims can help reconcile and heal these conflicts. Our government is beginning to invite representatives of our communities to play a role in mediating between the United States and the Muslim world. The more rapidly we develop a clear articulation of American Islam and define ourselves not as foreign imports, but as proudly *American* Muslims—both authentically *American* and authentically *Muslim*—the more powerful a force we can be for increasing understanding between our home country and the entire Muslim world.

By creating, defining, and shaping an American Islam, American Muslims can both integrate into the larger culture and society of their home country, and heal the modern, unnecessary, and dangerous divide between the West and the Muslim world. The Islam coming out of the West, which I have sketched in this book, true to Islam's origins and history, could have a revivalist effect on the rest of the Muslim world.

In the years just after 9/11 I used to think that those of us working to bridge the divide fundamentally failed to make our voices heard. But the truth is that little by little, over time, we actually have made a difference. We may not have had the immediate impact we wanted to have. After all, we had limited resources and capacity. But American Muslims have developed a following in the Muslim world, often at the highest levels of government—among presidents and prime ministers—who find this Shariah-informed message of nonviolence, tolerance, human rights, and social development enormously important as they confront the twenty-first century. They want to know how to develop their societies and build modern communities, making sure that people have what they need. And they want to be able to express these values and actions in the vocabulary of Islam. Because I speak about these matters from the point of view of the theological and legal imperatives of Islamic law and jurisprudence, I am invited repeatedly to speak throughout the Muslim world.

The impact of these ideas is being felt in the shifting of the Islamic political parties away from a focus on merely First Commandment issues (focusing on piety and observance of the rules of worship) to Second Commandment (Golden Rule) issues, which emphasize justice, economic and intellectual development, and people's quality of life.

There is also increasing understanding that the real fault line in global religion and politics is not that between the Muslim world and the West, but rather between political and religious moderates of all faiths and persuasions and extremists of all faiths and persuasions. Moderate Muslims, Jews, Christians, and atheists have far more in common with each other than they do with the extremists of their own faith or persuasion. The more we realize this commonality of values and beliefs, the less likely we will be to take the extremists and fundamentalists associated with any particular religion—al-Qaeda, say, or the Dove World Outreach Center—as genuine representatives of the religion. We will in effect have robbed extremists of their power to provoke murderous responses from each other.

American Muslims have a critical role to play, not only in this country, but in the world as a whole, in what I hope will become a global coalition of nonviolence and moderation. For the American expression of Islam is a powerfully moderate religion. With the exception of a small number of high-profile plots and attacks and the at times radical history of the Nation of Islam, American Muslims have relatively little history of extremism and no hierarchy or government ministry that can enforce a particular interpretation of Islam and Islamic law. Precisely because Islam is a minority religion in America, surrounded by large populations of Christians and Jews and atheists (unlike most of the Muslim world), we can model the very interfaith respect and practice envisioned in the Quran that used to exist far more widely in the Muslim world.

Here in America we Muslims are learning what it means to practice our faith in a dynamic, pluralistic, egalitarian, open, and (mostly) tolerant society. We are gaining national and worldwide attention as musicians, athletes, entertainers, journalists, writers, and politicians. We are developing a generation of religious leaders who are exploring how Islam can adapt itself to the American context while remaining true to Shariah and the core principles of our faith. American Muslim women are rising to leadership positions within the Muslim community and are beginning to have a global impact on such issues as interfaith marriage, combating female genital cutting, and the training of *muftiyyah*s and Shariah court judges.

To paraphrase my astute questioner from the days after 9/11: What can a good Christian, Jew, or Muslim do?

I remain profoundly convinced that practical multifaith projects are the single best vehicles for Jews, Christians, and Muslims to form the bonds that can build an American faith-based coalition of moderates. Muslims need to incorporate the reality of our theological, historical, and experiential connections to Christians and Jews into our lives and religious practice.

If you attend a mosque, speak to the imam about creating common projects with a local Christian and/or Jewish congregation. They are, after all, fellow People of the Book. You could suggest reading Scriptures together, or exploring common history, or comparing attitudes toward social justice. You could suggest inviting them to break the fast with you one Ramadan evening. If you are Jewish or Christian, invite your Muslim neighbors to join you on Yom Kippur to break the fast or to celebrate communion.

The more we experience others practicing their religion, the more we will all appreciate our core similarities. We need to take the lead in doing everything we can to undermine the growing Islamophobia in the United States. The worst thing we can do is keep to ourselves and refuse to engage the larger culture. This will only continue to make us seem strange, clannish, and foreign, unduly influenced by "radical Islamists" abroad. I know this is a tall order. But we have some powerful, principled, and influential friends. Many Jewish and Christian clergy have taken morally and ethically courageous stands in favor of Muslims' right to religious practice and religious freedom.

Many politicians, including Presidents George W. Bush and Barack Obama, Mayor Michael Bloomberg, and Governor Chris Christie of New Jersey, have done so as well. They deserve the nation's and the Muslim community's deepest thanks and praise. Ordinary Americans too have been our allies: I have an enormous *Eid Mubarak* (Blessed End of Ramadan) card prominently displayed in my office, signed by hundreds of members of a downtown Jewish synagogue in the midst of the Cordoba House crisis in 2010.

Traditional American values of religious tolerance and freedom do not support Islamophobia. The welcome to immigrants symbolized by the Statue of Liberty is tendered to Muslims as well. The Constitution of the United States guarantees our freedom of religious and political expression. The laws of this great land protect our right to practice Shariah—God's law—every single day.

We need to stand tall, claim our status as part of the American tapestry, and build on the reservoir of goodwill we already have in this country. I can assure you, from my experience in the days and weeks after 9/11, that even Americans who felt directly attacked by Islam wanted to understand Muslims better, wanted better relationships with Muslims, wanted a better relationship with the Muslim world.

When we build new mosques, let us have architectural competitions for a genuinely American design instead of endlessly repeating the designs of medieval Cairo or Istanbul. Let us invite American designers to design fashionable hijabs and fashionably modest clothing for American Muslim men and women, and take advantage of an entirely new market. We could publicize these designs through our societies and our mosques. There is no end to the ways we can embrace American institutional and cultural forms, from architecture to food, home design to gardening. The JWT marketing agency estimated the U.S. Muslim consumer market at roughly $170 billion in 2007. By using just a fraction of those dollars to purchase products that bridge contemporary Muslim and American ideas and trends, we could make a real contribution both to the integration of our community into the larger American culture and to the enrichment of American culture itself.

Moreover by engaging with our Jewish and Christian brothers and sisters, we will not only enrich our own lives; we will fulfill God's commandment in the Quran (42:13): "Be not divided therein." The truth is, for all of the Quranic emphasis on our common Abrahamic origins, few Muslims ever read the Torah, Psalms, or Gospels, *which we consider divinely inspired.* By making these connections, by undertaking projects together, we will help our children grow up in a more tolerant and peaceful nation and world.

No matter your religion, whatever influence you can bring to bear on making a Middle East peace will be repaid tenfold in decreasing the tensions between Muslims and Jews worldwide. As I have written, the open wound of the Israeli-Palestinian conflict will poison the relationship between Muslims and Jews for as long as there is no peace. All of us need to recognize that the status quo is unsustainable, endangers everyone in the world, and forces ordinary Israelis and Palestinians into a profoundly insecure existence. A global coalition of nonviolent, moderate Christians, Jews, and Muslims could have enormous moral authority in bringing the parties to a genuine peace table to hammer out a just settlement that does not give in to the extremist positions on all sides of the conflict. The great masses of people in the Middle East want peace; they need the assistance of principled moderates of all faiths in making it. American Jews and Muslims would have disproportionate influence in such a genuine peace process.

For those of you who belong to a church, synagogue, or temple, especially in a city, the chances are these days that there is a mosque not far away. You may already participate in an annual interfaith Thanksgiving service with Muslims, but there is much more you can do to help forge the kinds of bonds we need to undermine Islamophobia in the United States. You will find your Muslim neighbors extremely eager to undertake projects with you and to begin the process of bridge building. You might suggest a study group on key passages from the

Bible and the Quran, or a Memorial Day barbecue cook-off, or a breaking of the fast during Ramadan. You could assemble an Abrahamic softball or bowling or volleyball team for local leagues. You could put together an Abrahamic group for outings to the theater or the summer music festival or Labor Day picnic, Fourth of July parade, or the local major or minor league baseball game. You could ask a local imam or congregational leader to give the opening prayer or lead the Pledge of Allegiance at meetings of the City Council or local Kiwanis or Rotary meeting. These may sound like small acts, but they all chip away at the mountain of distrust and ignorance that leave all of us more vulnerable to the siren songs of extremism and Islamophobia.

But we need more, of course. The problems besetting us span the globe, which is why we need to rally moderates in faith communities worldwide who are willing to undertake truly nonviolent solutions. If you think this is an impractical dream, consider the evidence of 2011's Arab Winter, Spring, Summer, and Fall. Surprising pundits and governments, millions of ordinary Muslims and Christians, as well as political and religious leaders of all kinds, turned conventional wisdom upside down and risked their lives, fortunes (no matter how small), and sacred honor on behalf of a more just and democratic present and future.

Those of us in the Abrahamic faith traditions, along with those of us who set their sights by the Second Commandment, the Golden Rule, have the spiritual resources to move mountains, heal global conflict, and reclaim God's religion from extremists. Just as America has had a powerful effect on the entire globe, especially through its Declaration of Independence and Statue of Liberty, American Muslims, by articulating and embracing an authentic, moderate, nonviolent, compassionate, tolerant American Islam, can help trigger a worldwide renaissance in genuine Islamic values and help bring peace, justice, and mercy to our troubled world.

ACKNOWLEDGMENTS

Moving the Mountain is the result of a half century of study, reflection, struggle, and engagement with my faith, as well as a lifetime of experience in a wide variety of Muslim communities in the United States and all over the world. It also comes out of my intellectual, personal, spiritual, and organizational interactions with Jews, Christians, Hindus, Buddhists, and adherents of many other faiths, as well as agnostics and atheists.

The ideal of religious tolerance came under enormous pressure in the summer of 2010, as the controversy over Cordoba House in lower Manhattan took on feverish intensity. In the midst of that crisis, thousands of political and religious leaders across the political and religious spectrum, public officials, advocates, journalists, lawyers, filmmakers, comedians, 9/11 communities, and ordinary citizens, religious and secular, stood up for the principles of religious freedom against the forces of fear and hatred—here and abroad. I only know a small portion of these people, but even so it would take pages to thank them all by name here. So let me address you directly. I know that many of you paid a heavy price for your public stands. I honor and thank you for your courage. Your support inspired me to write this book.

Thanks to Richard Levick, who helped me think through this book in its early stages, and to the wonderful writer James Carroll, who urged me to write a book while interviewing me for the *New York Times Magazine*. I was exceptionally fortunate to have as my literary agent the remarkable Wendy Strothman, whose efforts on behalf of her clients are becoming the stuff of legend. She helped shape this book, gave chapters careful readings, and, most of all, found it the right home at Free Press. There, this book and I both benefited immensely from the enthusiasm, guidance, and editorial skills of Alessandra Bastagli. I also thank copyeditor Judith Hoover for working magic on my prose throughout the book.

I thank Ali Karjooravary for his patient scholarly efforts locating references. Special thanks to my dear friends Kurt Tolksdorf, Dr. Abu Baker Shingieti, and Naz Ahmed Georgas, who took the time out of their own very full lives to read this book in draft form and offer vigorous, helpful criticism and support.

Because my dear wife and partner, Daisy Khan, believes deeply in the vision articulated in *Moving the Mountain,* she patiently (well, mostly patiently) put up with me while I wrote it. Since she is an extraordinarily astute writer and editor in her own right, as well as my best critic, I am immensely grateful for the time she took out of her work and our life together to read and critique the entire manuscript. Of course, I take responsibility for any errors that remain.

At the deepest level, this book comes out of my life journey, so my final thanks are to my dear mother, Buthayna Ayad Rauf, and my late father, Dr. Muhammad Abdul Rauf; my teachers; and the colleagues, students, and friends from whom I learned so much. It is this learning that I have sought to share in these pages. May God shower blessings on them all.

NOTES

4 "seek knowledge as far as China": This widely cited *hadith* may be found in Bayhaqi, *Shu'ub al-iman.*

21 Less than five months after assuming office: "As a citizen and as president, I believe that Muslims have the same right to practice their religion as everyone else in this country," Mr. Obama said. "That includes the right to build a place of worship and a community center on private property in lower Manhattan, in accordance with local laws and ordinances." *CBS News,* August 13, 2010.

30 a story by the thirteenth-century poet Rumi: Rumi story, "Two Friends," in *The Essential Rumi,* trans. Coleman Barks (New York, 1995), 87–88.

42 Never have I witnessed such sincere hospitality: Malcolm X and Alex Haley, *The Autobiography of Malcolm X* (New York, 1965), 346–47.

46 Or, as the Jewish teacher Hillel answered: Babylonian Talmud, tractate Shabbat, folio 31a.

66 an op-ed piece for the local newspaper: *The Star* (Kuala Lumpur), July 29, 2009.

67 "brutal application of Shariah law, whereas in fact it was a *violation*": Jack Healy, "In Afghanistan, Rage at Young Lovers," *New York Times,* July 30, 2011. For the earlier killing, see Rod Nordland, "In Bold Display, Taliban Order Stoning Deaths," *New York Times,* August 16, 2010.

69 The Prophet himself forgave a man . . . forgave the city: Ibn Kathir, *Tareekh.*

70 In the United States alone: Material on the death penalty may be found in "Facts about the Death Penalty, Updated October 21, 2011," Death Penalty Information Center, as well as on the website of the organization, www.deathpenaltyinfo.org.

76 only four had minarets: Nick Cumming-Bruce and Steven Erlanger, "Swiss Ban Building of Minarets on Mosques, " *New York Times,* November 29, 2009

92 Rumi tells a funny story: "Moses and the Shepherd," in *The Essential Rumi,* 165–67.

109 Caliph Umar's conversion to Islam: Ibn Ishaq, *Seerah.*

111 women's rights and opportunities are: World Economic Forum, *The Global Gender Gap Report 2010;* "Muslim Women Gain Higher Profile in U.S.," *New York Times,* December 27, 2010;

111 higher education levels: Gallup for Muslim studies, *Muslim Americans: A National Portrait. An In-depth Analysis of America's Most Diverse Religious Community,* 2009.

113 No contemporary Islamic scholar, not even the most extreme: Tun Abdul Hamid Mohamed, "Harmonization of Common Law and Shariah in Malaysia: A Practical Approach," *Malaysian Law Journal* 2 (2009).

127 As she put on her traditional robe before landing: James Zogby, *Arab Voices: What They Are Saying to Us, and Why It Matters* (New York, 2010), 5.

138 some 58,000 people were killed or injured: U.S. Department of State, National Counterterrorism Center, *Annex of Statistical Information,* August 5, 2010.

140 "Islam has bloody borders": Samuel P. Huntington, "The Clash of Civilizations," *Foreign Affairs,* Summer 1993.

142 even regarded Islam as a Christian heresy: In "the mid-eighth century . . . John of Damascus . . . a high administrator for the Umayyads . . . wrote his famous treatise on 'The *Heresy* of the Ishmaelites.' In other words, he could still perceive nascent Islam as a form of Christian heresy, rather than as a fully independent religion." Fred M. Don-

ner, *Muhammad and the Believers: At the Origins of Islam* (Cambridge, Mass., 2010), 223.

152 in January 2012: "PM: Global Movement of Moderates Foundation to be launched Jan 2012," *The Star* (Kuala Lumpur), November 13, 2011

154 Khan taught, preached, and practiced nonviolence: Eknath Easwaran, *Nonviolent Soldier of Islam: Badshah Khan, a Man to Match His Mountains, 2nd edition* (Tomales, Calif., 1999), 13.

156 would four blocks also be acceptable, or eight?: Clyde Haberman, "Near Ground Zero, the Sacred and the Profane," *New York Times*, May 27, 2010.

157 Mayor Michael Bloomberg said: "Bloomberg: Moving Mosque Would 'Compromise Our Commitment to Fighting Terror with Freedom,'" *New York Magazine*, August 24, 2010. For other Jewish support, see "Some Jewish activists support Ground Zero mosque in NYC, *USA Today*," August 8, 2010. For Christian support, see Gene Davenport, "On Faith," *Washington Post*, July 19, 2010.

157 A friend of mine in Egypt called me excitedly: "Obama OKs Mosque Plan Near Ground Zero," *Egyptian Gazette*, August 14, 2010.

159 or Khariji Islam (to use Islamic vocabulary): The Kharijites were an extremist, even terrorist group in the seventh and eighth centuries that developed a radical theology allowing them to kill anyone who disagreed with them.

175 I have been given authority over you: Ibn Hisham, *Seerah*.

177 In one of his best-known sayings on the importance of justice: Ibn Taymiyya, *Majmu' al-Fatawa*, 28/146.

191 "Rear your children for a time different from your own.": Ibn Abi al-Hadid 20:102.

193 about the high school football teams in Dearborn, Michigan: Jere Longman, "All-Nighters for a Football Team during Ramadan," *New York Times*, August 10, 2010.

198 the Muslim consumer market at roughly $170 billion: Louise Story, "U.S. Advertisers Reach Out to Muslim Consumers," *New York Times*, April 27, 2010.

GLOSSARY OF ARABIC WORDS USED IN THE TEXT

adhan: The Muslim call to prayer, given by a muezzin.

bay'ah: literally, "to give allegiance." *Bay'ah* represents the consent of the governed to those who govern them.

caliph: from Arabic *khalifatu rasul Allah,* literally "successor of the Messenger of God." The term used by Muslims to designate their early political leaders. The four immediate successors of the Prophet were called "the rightly guided caliphs" to distinguish them from the general corruption of political affairs that came after their reign. These four are Abu Bakr, Umar, Uthman, and Ali.

dhikr: literally, "remembrance," a shortened form of *dhikr ullah* (remembrance of God). All forms of worship are also acts of remembering God. The most important form of *dhikr* is repeating the *shahada* and God's names. Sufi masters have composed special litanies of *dhikr* for their followers.

din: religion, law. Islam is a *din* that is made up of three dimensions: submission, faith, and virtue.

fatwa: a legal opinion given by a mufti (Latin, a *prudent*) in accordance with Islamic law.

fiqh: literally, "understanding," a shortened form of *fiqh al-shariah* (the understanding of God's ordinances). This refers to the human interpretation and development of God's laws into jurisprudence.

Hadith: literally, "happening" or "news." A *hadith* is a report of something the Prophet said or did. Sunni and Shia Muslims developed their own *Hadith* literature, with Sunni Muslims adhering to a main corpus of six collections and Shia Muslims adhering to a corpus of four collections.

hajj: "pilgrimage." One of the five pillars of Islam. Muslims who are physically and financially able are obliged to make pilgrimage to the Kaaba, a cube-shaped temple devoted to God, located in the city of Mecca in what is today Saudi Arabia. Muslims believe that this temple was built by Abraham.

halal: "permissible," the opposite of *haraam,* "forbidden," and referring to actions permitted or forbidden by God. All actions that are not *haraam* are de facto *halal.* The expression "*halal* food" means food that contains nothing forbidden for Muslims to consume, such as any pork product (bacon, ham) or meat from an animal slaughtered in a way that violates Islamic law.

hijab: literally, "veil." The hijab is commonly used to describe the head coverings or headscarves that many Muslim women wear.

imam: the person who leads the Muslim congregational prayer. Among Sunnis, the term Imam has been used historically to refer to notable religious scholars or founders of the Sunni schools of jurisprudence. Among Shias, the term is additionally used to refer to their twelve most important political leaders starting with Imam Ali, the cousin and son-in-law of the Prophet.

khalifa: "successor or vice regent." The Quran quotes God as announcing He has established human beings as His successors or vice regents (*khalifas*) on earth. See "caliph," the anglicized version of this word.

mosque: from Arabic *masjid,* literally "place of prostration."

muezzin: the caller of the *adhan,* the Muslim call to prayer.

mufti, f. *muftiyyah*: literally, "one who issues fatwas." The Muslim adaptation of the Roman *prudent,* who would issue a legal opinion to educate his townsfolk on an issue of law. A mufti or *muftiyyah* issues legal opinions, and teaches what is Islamically right or wrong to his or her constituency.

People of the Book: Arabic *ahl al-kitab,* the Quranic way of addressing or referring to non-Muslim faith communities that received a scripture from God. The Quran affirms that Christians and Jews were given divine scriptures. The term has been extended by Muslims to other faith communities whom they believe received an authentic divine revelation.

Quran: literally, "the recitation," the scripture of Muslims. Muslims accept the Quran as the word of God, authored by God and revealed to the Prophet Muhammad over a period of twenty-three years. The Quran is distinguished from the *Hadith,* which are the Prophet's own words.

shahada: literally, "witnessing." The testimony of faith of Islam: "I bear witness that there is no god but God and I bear witness that Muhammad is God's Messenger."

Shariah: from the word *shar',* which means "ordinance," referring to God's ordinances, defined as the approximately 500 Quranic commandments and 1,200 prophetic commandments. Although the term *fiqh al-shariah* (or *fiqh* for short, the understanding of the divine ordinances) refers to the collective fourteen centuries of human interpretation and development of its jurisprudence, the term "Shariah" is also loosely used by Muslims to refer generally to the entire corpus of Islamic law. The four sources of the law are the Quran, the *Hadith,* Consensus, and Reasoning by Analogy.

Shia: from Arabic, *shi'atu 'Ali,* the partisans or disciples of Ali, who believe that the Prophet directly appointed his son in-law Ali to be his successor, and that legitimate leadership of the community comes only through the direct blood-line of Ali. They are the non-Sunni Muslims who comprise 15 percent of the Muslim world, and live predominantly in the countries ringing the Persian Gulf such as Iran, Iraq and Bahrain, but constitute important minorities in other countries such as the eastern region of Saudi Arabia, Afghanistan, Pakistan, and Lebanon.

Sufism: The esoteric or inner tradition of Islam, shared by Sunnis and Shias, which focuses on spirituality, the refinement and awakening of the heart. People who enter a Sufi order (*tariqa*) are guided by a *shaykh* (a spiritual guide) along this path of inner development through the prescription of litanies of divine remembrance (*dhikr*) handed down from the Prophet and Sufi masters and guides. The goal of the Sufi path is the "unveiling of God," the experiential vision of His face.

sunna: literally, "tradition," from *sunnatu rasulillah,* "the tradition of the messenger of God." A term used by all Muslims to refer to the normative precedents and example of the Prophet, whom they take as the model for both their religious and worldly lives. Muslims therefore follow the Prophet's sunna in how they pray, fast, perform the rites of pilgrimage; they also ask themselves, "What would the Prophet do?" and seek to emulate his worldly practices, such as washing his hands before and after eating, brushing his teeth, how he behaved with his wives and family, how he was charitable to others.

Sunni: from Arabic, *ahl al-sunnah wa-l jama'a,* "the people of tradition and the majority." The major non-Shia group of Muslims today, making up 85 percent of the Muslim world. They believe that the Prophet did not appoint a successor and that leadership of the community is to be decided by the community. They initially chose Abu Bakr, the Prophet's closest and best friend and one of the elders among the companions, to succeed the Prophet.

Wahhabism: A puritan and fundamentalist interpretation of Islam that began in the eighteenth century in the Najd region of eastern Saudi Arabia, and which has been dominant in Saudi Arabia since the mid-twentieth century. Because of Saudi Arabia's considerable financial clout, especially since 1973, combined with its control over the two sacred sites of Mecca and Medina (the king of Saudi Arabia has assumed the title Custodian—or Servant—of the two Sacred Sites), Wahhabism has acquired widespread influence in the Muslim world.

zakat: one of the five pillars of Islam, an alms tax ranging from 2.5 to 20 percent of one's income (depending on the source of the income), to be paid to charity or to the state for charitable and specific other needs. Some scholars believe that the modern income tax satisfies the requirement of *zakat*.

INDEX

ABOUT THE AUTHOR

Imam Feisal Abdul Rauf is founder and CEO of the Cordoba Initiative, Imam of the al-Farah mosque since 1983, and the visionary behind Cordoba House, the interfaith religious and community center close to the site of the former World Trade Center. The author of three previous books about Islam, an American goodwill ambassador abroad, and a sought-after speaker and media guest, he is committed to building bridges between America and the Muslim world, and between American Muslims and other Americans. He lives in New York City.